Beautiful Flowers of the Maquiladora

Translations from Latin America Series

Beautiful Flowers of the Maquiladora
Life Histories of Women Workers in Tijuana

By Norma Iglesias Prieto
Translated by Michael Stone with Gabrielle Winkler
Foreword by Henry Selby

University of Texas Press, Austin
Institute of Latin American Studies

Translation copyright © 1997 by the University of Texas Press
Printed in the United States of America

First University of Texas Press Edition, 1997

∞ The paper used in this publication meets the minimum requirements of American National Standard for Information Sciences—Permanence of Paper for Printed Library Materials, ANSI Z39.48–1984.

Library of Congress Cataloging-in-Publication Data

Iglesias Prieto, Norma
  [Flor más bella de la maquiladora. English]
  Beautiful flowers of the maquiladora : life histories of women workers in Tijuana / by Norma Iglesias Prieto : translated by Michael Stone with Gabrielle Winkler : foreword by Henry Selby.
    p. cm. — (Translations from Latin America Series)
  Includes bibliographical references and index.
  ISBN 0-292-73868-4 (cloth : alk. paper). — ISBN 0-292-73869-2 (pbk. : alk. paper)
  1. Women offshore assembly industry workers—Mexico—Tijuana (Baja California Norte)—Interviews. 2. Women—Employment—Mexico—Tijuana (Baja California Norte). 3. Women—Mexico—Tijuana (Baja California Norte)—Economic conditions. I. Title. II. Series.
HD6073.0332M495513 1997
331.4'87042'09721—dc21   97-13339

Centuries of social, economic, and political disadvantage; grandmothers, mothers, and daughters who are born, live, and die confined to the four walls of the home; women subject to the authority of their fathers, spouses, and even their sons; the reality of an education truncated by work at wages inferior to men's; entire lives whose reality is conditioned by tradition and legend, textbook definitions, and the manifold bombardment of the mass media devised to signify women's inferior status and ensure their insecurity and disregard—all this has its cost.

—Margaret Randall
"La mujer: especificidad de su problemática,"
in *El Día*

Contents

Foreword

I had occasion to visit a Japanese-managed, American-owned maquiladora in the Piedras Negras area a couple of years ago with a Japanese graduate student who had spent about three months studying how the place functioned. Because I was a gray-haired professor from the main campus of the state university, they thought I could talk to them about important things, such as how they could cut their very high turnover rate. "Increase wages," said I, although I would have said the same had they asked me how they could curtail absenteeism—or cure boils, for that matter. A sad look came over the manager, who owned that this was quite impossible because the union had forbidden it.

The maquiladora produced Disneyesque figurines, which sold for $20 in Chicago, and could be produced for less than a dollar in the maquiladora. "Praying Hands" was their best-seller; it did terribly well both in Cleveland and in the Greater Chicago area. They had their own designers, who made copies of Disney figures, and the nimble hands of young women who fashioned the offspring of the Seven Dwarfs.

Incredible profit margins motivated manufacturing, but only with very cheap labor and efficient use of modern technology could the trade be sufficiently profitable to engage the interest of wholesalers in the United States. There were no sales in Mexico. There was fear in the managers' eyes as they talked about competition from China— "Competencia desleal."

Morals were an important facet of maquiladora life, as the "morals officer," a middle-aged woman of somewhat prim features assured me. "The young women would all become prostitutes if we let them," she explained (although no one had inquired about the probable destinies of the workers sans maquiladora), "so we make sure that they are escorted to and from their jobs, and are kept in a woman's dormitory, five to a room." I tried to go into the dormitory, but was ejected with catcalls from the top floor while being advised that I was indeed a male, and therefore undesirable. My graduate student had lived in one of the apartments and said that it was really okay, but that the *muchachas* kept turning off their air conditioning because of the noise it made.

I cannot say that I wasn't prepared for all this, for I had read with tremendous interest a book by Norma Iglesias called *La flor más bella de la maquiladora* just after it was published in 1985. Some conditions have changed since the publication of the book, but most have not. Wages have gone down, not up, as a result of the devaluation and the deterioration of the peso under President Zedillo's administration. The workforce has been "masculinized" as more and more men have become available because of high unemployment. Men have acquired nimble fingers in direct proportion to the loss of the ability to protest and organize for collective bargaining. During the period the book was being written, Mexican men were viewed as more likely to cause trouble, to go on strike, to agitate for higher wages and better working conditions. This is no longer true. Male militancy was another casualty of the never-ending Mexican crisis; now men are as harmless as women ever were, and therefore can be rehired. Their unions are now as completely at the beck and call of the state as they ever have been, and employers have lost all fear of labor mobilizations.

The unemployment situation in Mexico has worsened greatly since the writing of the book. Open unemployment has reached unprec-edented levels, near 6 percent, which is astonishing in a country that lacks a safety net. Underemployment, consisting of substandard wages, or part-time work where full-time is required, is also at an all-time high. NAFTA has been a disaster for the ordinary working Mexican, aside from those who are fortunate enough to get a job in transnational corpora-tions. Intermediate and small-scale industry in Mexico was crushed not just by NAFTA, but by the ideologically driven opening of the economy to foreign imports under the General Agreement on Tariffs and Trade (GATT). The best-known example is that of the shoe industry, which was decimated by cheap imports; shoe production, especially in the workshops that had supported many families in the west of Mexico, was gone, it seemed, overnight.

Why has Mexico not responded with worker militancy and political mobilizations, then? One answer is given by Jorge Castañeda, who points out that, one way or another, 25 percent of Mexico's families are living in a "dollarized" world in which an important part of their income is tied to the U.S. economy. The two most important sectors are tourism and the maquiladoras. So one-quarter of Mexico's families are not affected by Mexico's economic woes and pray not for a revaluation of the peso as much as a continuing overvaluation of the dollar, which will permit them to live better on their dollarized incomes.

Castañeda goes on to point out something that became increasingly clear during the Salinas years also: the United States, partly because of NAFTA, and partly because of U.S. racism, which foments dark fears of being invaded by illegal immigrants, is now responsible for the Mexican economy. The U.S. government stopped bothering to justify Mexican bailouts, since their value was so obvious to the United States. As a result of the last "bridge loan" arranged by the United States, the discount rate on Mexican debt rose dramatically. All of a sudden Mexican debt was worth a great deal more than it had been. So Salinas succeeded where all his predecessors had failed. Not only did he make the United States pay attention to Mexico, but he succeeded in making the United States responsible for the Mexican economy. Thus, the most corrupt one-party rule in the Americas is being continually bailed out by the United States, with never a question asked.

American taxpayers may be irritated at their funds' being used to pay off the dollar billionaires, like Emilio Azcárraga, but the effect is more than irritating to the Mexican opposition. Uncle Sam is sticking Mexicans with the real cost, the cost of having a PRI-dominated administration for the foreseeable future. Responsibility for Mexican economic and political process is now squarely in the hands of the gringos, and the Mexicans can do nothing.

One of the things I increasingly admire in social critics is their unwillingness to label agents of the system as bad guys. It's the system that is rotten, not the middle-level management types, who may or may not benefit from it. And that is true in Iglesias's account, too. There is a love-hate relationship between the women and their jobs. They need the money, they hate the work. Their only recourse is to quit, and they do, in droves. The conditions under which they work are bad: days without sun, breathing acid fumes, with no protective gear, with near-electrocutions, with polluted spaces on the job and around the home, with constant demands to intensify the production process. These make the boring and dangerous work nearly impossible.

Perhaps the most frustrating part of their situation is that often "they don't know for whom they work, or the uses of the product they manufacture, what value it might have. In the majority of cases they do not even know the owner of the company." There is no one concrete to fight against; it is a fight against another octopus, another "*pulpo*," this time not the official political party or the bureaucracy, but seemingly acephalous transnational corporations.

To me the most telling part of the story is the rending account of the mechanisms of control, tales of ideology, discourse, and hegemony in the current anthropological dispensation. The plants have in-house fiestas, factory trips to exotic places like Ensenada, dances, dinners, raffles, beauty pageants, walks, country outings, and sports. Stratagems include becoming the boss's pet without having sex with him, flirting to become a supervisor, and so on. It's a good thing the workers are sexually so protected, or they would be more vulnerable to the unwelcome advances of predatory foremen. The whole notion that the maquiladora is some kind of (patriarchal, authoritarian) family in which *muchachas* do well to mind their betters, just as they minded their fathers and brothers, is inculcated in daily practices.

The writing is superb, and the translation by Michael Stone and Gabrielle Winkler is excellent. One of the hardest things to do is to render dialogue across cultures, particularly with poor people who speak a kind of "village Spanish," as so many of the girls in the maquiladora do. Bad translations render them in a kind of Tonto English, which makes them come off sounding stupid because the translator doesn't know how to render the dialect. A lot of translators have people saying things like, "Yes, life is hard, but it is beautiful to know everything." This is a typical village "phatic" banality, equivalent to "esteeeeee," or the American English "You know what I mean?" Stone and Winkler never do that in their translation, and the young women come across very much as they are. They retain the workers' dignity and their point of view, as well as the freshness of their voices. Now English readers have a wonderful text on a terrible, but important, subject.

—*Henry A. Selby*

Translators' Foreword

In the twentieth century the United States has often exported its domestic social predicaments to the so-called Third World. The peripatetic character of late capitalism is perhaps nowhere more apparent than in the urban cultural tangle of the U.S.-Mexico border's twin cities, and in the maquiladoras that have engendered a contingent work force whose compound vulnerability is a key element of latter-day industrial productivity. But labor vulnerability also travels without a passport, as INS authorities, anti-immigration vigilantes, employers of the undocumented, "English-only" advocates, "deskilled" workers, and all those who tremble at NAFTA's "giant sucking sound" are edgily aware.

The bilateral accord that opened the way in the mid-1960s for these transnational assembly plants triggered unprecedented migration from Mexico's rural interior to its urbanizing northern frontier. But it also marked the inauguration of U.S. job exports, and the long decline of a North American labor aristocracy after the "oil shock" of 1973. By the end of that decade Norma Iglesias Prieto had already begun to document the myriad impact of transnational enterprise and global economic restructuring just south of the border. But apart from cheaper home electronics and celebrity sweatshop ready-wear, an awareness of the fuller and more paradoxical implication for workers and consumers in the north has been slower to register.

The maquiladoras have emerged as a prominent structural feature of the U.S.-Mexico frontier over the past 30 years, and stand as the prototype for what David Harvey[1] sees as a corporate shift from Fordism to a global regime of flexible accumulation. Iglesias Prieto was among the first researchers to approach the maquiladora as a site of social, economic, and political struggle over the everyday toll of that fundamental transformation. She queried the presumed benefits these enterprises held out to their laborers, and interrogated the palpable social disparities reproduced in these "offshore" economic enclaves. The conditions she documented approximate, for better or worse, those that growing numbers of wage-earners confront today, in the United States as in much of the rest of the world.

Iglesias Prieto also wrote at a time when the matter of textual production was unburdened by a full appreciation of the complex, problematic presumption to speak for those whom Salvadoran Archbishop Oscar Arnulfo Romero fatefully embraced as "*los sin voz.*" And here is the dilemma. In acting to give voice to those Eric Wolf[2] has called "the people without history," social science maintains an unavoidably ambiguous relationship with the everyday strife that animates all history in the vivid conditions of its making. To truly speak, and to speak truly, is no longer to speak for, but to stand with. Standing at a remove from the subject of its genesis and sustenance, every text demands analysis—deliberation—in its transcription, production, translation, and reading. But intellectuals all should never mistake that deliberation for the flesh-and-blood stirrings it presumes to represent and analyze.

Memories of the Spanish spoken, the sound and substance of life along the border and in Mexico's interior, have inspired the process of these testimonies' transliteration. But to interpret a multivocal text such as this, a singular artifact of the contradictory and mundane intentions of exploitation, antithetical scholarship, and the subjects' often contradictory affirmation of their own humanity, to render these women's already mediated utterances in an English resonant with the character of voices not silenced, but never heard by translator or reader, to emancipate the cross-cutting intentions of this project of many and disparate articulations—this has been our necessarily fugitive task. And the summary irony is that whatever this layered communiqué may reveal, what it fails to render runs far deeper. Provisioned and clothed, surrounded by the production of their hands and their lives, complicit in their exploitation through patterns of consumption, mutual-fund investments, retirement funds, and an acquiescence to U.S. immigration policy, we "know" the fates of these women and their families by an abstraction that offers no comfort to those for whom this work presumes in all goodwill to "speak."

At ILAS, we owe special thanks to Virginia Hagerty and Carolyn Palaima for recognizing the vitality of Norma Iglesias Prieto's work and for seeing us through the course of its translation. Also at ILAS, Anne Dibble and Virginia Garrard-Burnett have been supporters, friends, and confidantes over the years. The early encouragement and enduring example of Don Américo Paredes remain an inspiration—border scholar *así no hay como dos.* Henry Selby first called his students' attention to this book more than a decade ago, and in that sense his endorsement accounts for its appearance now in English translation. Thanks to former ILAS director Peter Cleaves for helping to create the opportunity to teach there in 1994–95. His predecessor, Richard N. Adams, and Betty Hannstein Adams know better than anyone the profound influence they have had in both the translators' lives—for that we remain immensely grateful. And on the anniversary of her birth, this one is for Solana.

—Michael Stone and Gabrielle Winkler
March 1, 1997

Notes

1. David Harvey, *The Condition of Postmodernity: An Enquiry into the Origins of Cultural Change*. Cambridge, Mass., and Oxford, UK: Blackwell, 1990.

2. Eric Wolf, *Europe and the People without History*. Berkeley: University of California Press, 1982.

Acknowledgments

I am deeply grateful to the countless individuals who were involved at various stages of this work's development. First, I want to thank the working women who extended their friendship and gave of their valuable time so that I might carry out my research. I am indebted to Gabriela for having had confidence in this undertaking and for having opened her doors in the determination that working women's lives might be more profoundly understood.

I must also acknowledge Jorge Carrillo's support, without which this text would never have been realized. Thanks to Jorge A. Bustamente for his enthusiasm, economic assistance, and encouragement.

Elena Bilbao and Mónica Lavin offered valuable commentaries and critiques that were fundamental in tabulating, composing, and analyzing data. Thanks to Ricardo Falomir, Raúl Nieto, Andrés Fábregas, Patricia Fernández Kelly, and Gustavo del Castillo for their opportune considerations. Thanks to Juan Martinez, Lucía Sisniega, and Jorge Salazar for their interest in the work, their patience, and their moral support.

Thanks likewise to the members of the Sindicato Independiente Solidev Mexicana for their companionship and their concern. Thanks to Alejandrina Osuna for her patience and dedication in the computer editing of the Spanish-language text, and in general to all the personnel of El Colegio de la Frontera Norte for their support.

Finally, I would like to register my gratitude to Norma Prieto de Iglesias and Roberto Iglesias Hernández, as much for economic sustenance as the confidence, enthusiasm, and love they have shared with me, their daughter.

Introduction

Beginning in the 1970s, with the initiation of the Border Industrialization Program and the end of the *bracero* program, Mexico's northern frontier underwent considerable socioeconomic change. The industrial expansion effected by the establishment of maquiladoras in the border cities conferred a singular quality to urban life there.

Through the Border Industrialization Program the Mexican government sought to reduce the rising unemployment rate associated with the *bracero* program's termination. Instead of utilizing unemployed males, however, maquiladoras contracted a new labor force—single women between the ages of sixteen and twenty-four, with only primary-level education. The firms stood to benefit economically by employing these young women, whose docility, discipline, and good health promised increased productivity.

The hiring of women, while it has generated employment, has failed to offer even a partial solution to the overall problem of unemployment and underemployment in the border region. Throughout the region maquiladoras typically have employed a labor force that is 80 to 90 percent female. This fundamental characteristic has affected the occupational structure and sociocultural character of border cities, as it has the families of female workers.

This study seeks to present and analyze the significance and meaning of being a female maquiladora worker on the U.S.-Mexico border. It draws on data collected from 1972 to February 1982, when the peso was devalued from twenty-seven to thirty-eight pesos to the dollar. It is important to note that by early 1983, many of the practices presented here were being modified conspicuously. That year marks the beginning of a new era for maquiladoras, which clearly are expanding because of the devaluation and the Mexican government's support.

The ten stories presented in this work are typical of the lives of female maquiladora laborers. These stories focus on ten women's perceptions of their lives as workers and the changes they underwent after becoming maquiladora workers. The awareness and knowledge these women gained through involvement in the production process are basic to understanding the process of consciousness raising and the existence or absence of a workers' movement in the maquiladoras.

Utilizing female labor and employing women who previously had been excluded from industrial production—women whose social lives had been circumscribed by domestic responsibilities—has conditioned the form and content of labor organizing along the border. Labor movement experience in the maquiladoras has not been extensive. The youth and inexperience of the women involved in production, the characteristics of the labor force, and the politics and maneuvers of the maquiladoras are among the factors that conditioned the situation in the period under discussion.

This book is divided into seven chapters intended to illustrate a global phenomenon encompassing both the maquiladoras and the life experience of each of the workers. The data were assembled via participant observation and the collection of life histories, methodologies that provide direct and emotive information. While I might have evaluated the data by identifying analytical variables, I have approached the material in a way that retains the thought processes of the women interviewed. Therefore, each chapter presents its own variables and logic, and only those aspects most relevant to my thesis are analyzed.

Chapter 1 shows the different productive processes of the maquiladoras. It illustrates the fragmented nature of the production process, its suppression of creativity, its alienating character, and how this constrains human intellectual development. The fragmentation of the work process is not exclusive to the maquiladoras, but the first chapter makes evident the alienation that proceeds from the accelerated rhythms of production and the overall work routine.

The second chapter describes work conditions, the frequent dangers facing maquiladora laborers in the workplace, and the inattention to accident and occupational ailment prevention. It underscores the dehumanization that results from giving priority to production values rather than workers' health. It also reflects the hierarchical structure of the division of labor and how that hierarchy facilitates obtaining the maximum yield from production.

The third chapter clearly illustrates why maquiladoras employ female laborers on Mexico's northern frontier and, more generally, in all those countries where this type of industry exists. It also addresses the specific difficulties facing women as they enter the labor market.

Chapter 4 describes the characteristics of the labor force employed in the maquiladoras and the advantages the firms obtain by pursuing their employment policies.

Chapter 5 offers accounts of the place of origin of some of the workers we interviewed, their experiences during the migratory process, and the advantages, disadvantages, and changes they encountered in acclimating to working in a maquiladora.

The sixth chapter registers the countless ideological and political control mechanisms designed by the enterprises to maximize production and to avoid, or at least to retard, the workers' consciousness-raising, and thus to impede their organization and struggle. It shows how control mechanisms were designed specifically to control young women, as they constituted the vast majority of workers in maquiladoras.

The seventh chapter deals with the experiences of a female member of one of the two independent labor unions that arose in the maquiladoras. It is the account of a workers' movement of considerable significance to workers' struggles on the U.S.-Mexico border. This chapter also summarizes a number of the points outlined in the preceding chapters.

To conclude, the factors most relevant to the analysis of the role of working women in Tijuana's maquiladoras are reviewed. A methodological appendix includes the questionnaire utilized in the research and a thematic protocol for recording the life histories.

Case Selection

A variety of considerations influenced the selection of the ten cases presented here. Within the maquiladoras there are distinct hiring patterns, depending on the sector involved and the importance of the firm. In the electronics industry, work is preferentially offered to single women between the ages of sixteen and twenty-four, migrants who have resided for at least six months in the city, and nonstudents. The work experience of the job seeker is of little importance, because the learning period is quite brief, a matter of hours or, at most, one or two days.

In the textile industry, work is offered preferentially to women who are already skilled seamstresses; their experience enables them to work more rapidly and precisely. According to Mexico's secretary of labor, this is a skilled occupation; maquiladora seamstresses at times do not earn even the minimum wage, however, because they do piece work. Older women with work experience are more likely to be employed in the textile-related maquiladoras than in the electronics plants. The majority of textile workers have children, and many of the women are the sole household providers, which makes them more dependent on their employers.

Most cases presented here describe women who became wage workers at a young age and who "grew old" in the maquiladoras. Hence, they

harbored distinct impressions of the maquiladora work experience, and
their interpretation of the situation differed considerably from that of
younger women. The ten cases presented here exemplify aspects of the
core maquiladora work force. The principal variables considered in our
selection were age, marital status, and number of children; place of
origin and (for migrants) motivations for migrating to Tijuana; employment sector and the magnitude of the salary's contribution to the family
economy. Following are the ten selected cases:

Alma migrated as a young married woman with her six-member
family to the United States to work as a seamstress in a textile
factory. She lived here for two years as an undocumented worker
before relocating to Tijuana, where she works as a maquiladora
seamstress. Her spouse is underemployed, so her salary is fundamental to the household economy.

Amelia is a single mother, thirty years old, with four children. She
migrated to Tijuana in search of employment and is an electronics
worker and the sole household supporter.

Ángela, a forty-two-year-old woman with four children, came to
Tijuana when she separated from her spouse. She has worked for
thirteen years in the same electronics plant and is the sole support
of her household.

Concha, a thirty-five-year-old married woman and a migrant, had
to stop working three years before we interviewed her because she
had no one to care for her children. She has never been the sole
economic support of her family, but her income has been very
important in meeting household expenses.

Elena, twenty-five years old and a migrant, is married and has
children. She has abandoned maquiladora employment for extended periods, but has returned on at least five occasions. Her
salary is considered supplementary to meeting household expenses.

Gabriela, a twenty-six-year-old migrant, has worked approximately
eight years in the same electronics plant. She has labor union
experience and has been involved in various labor struggles. She
lives alone and, apart from supporting herself, has to send money
to her family in Acaponeta, Nayarit.

María Cristina, eighteen years old, arrived in Tijuana as a teenager
with her family in search of better living conditions. She has
worked for a year in a textile maquiladora, her only work experience. Her earnings go principally toward her personal expenses.

María Luisa, thirty-one years old, is married. She is a migrant with
twelve years' experience in eight maquiladoras. Her salary is
considered supplementary to meeting household expenses.

Marta, a sixteen-year-old girl living with her family, was born in Tijuana. She had been working for only one week in the maquiladora when she was interviewed. Her earnings go toward personal expenses.

Obdulia, seventeen years old, recently married and with one child, was born in Tijuana. Her salary is essential to meeting household expenses, although her spouse also contributes a fixed monthly amount.

Maquiladoras

Maquiladoras are those manufacturing plants established in Mexico that

a) are U.S. subsidiaries or contract affiliates under Mexican or foreign ownership;

b) are dedicated to the assembly of components, the processing of primary materials, or both, producing either intermediate or final products;

c) import most or all primary materials and components from the United States, and re-export the end products of the manufacturing process to the United States;

d) are labor-intensive. (Carrillo and Hernández 1982a: 1)

The introduction of maquiladoras in Mexican territory was initiated officially in 1965 under the Border Industrialization Program. Since then, foreign enterprises dedicated to the processing, assembly, and finishing of raw materials and intermediate goods have brought plants from the United States to the principal cities of Mexico's northern border with the objective of reducing production costs by capitalizing on the extremely low cost of local labor.

The establishment of maquiladoras in Mexico reflects a capitalist tendency that has developed since the 1960s and that has facilitated the geographic relocation of productive processes to the underdeveloped countries. This tendency had become evident by 1975, as thousands of firms from highly developed countries had transferred their operations partially or wholly to no fewer than thirty-nine countries in Africa, Asia, Latin America, and the Caribbean.

Since their introduction into Mexico, the maquiladora export plants have maintained high rates of growth. By early 1982 there were six hundred plants employing 122,799 persons, and by September 1996, 2,490 plants employed 788,205 persons (INEGI 1996).

Although maquiladoras have generated a considerable number of jobs and since 1972 have maintained high rates of job growth, these jobs have gone to young single women without work experience, that is, to a sector with no prior experience in the labor force. Their employment expands the economically active population and the availability of jobs, but maquiladora expansion has also fostered border population growth by attracting migrants to these industries, which elevates unemployment.

The establishment of maquiladoras in the northern border zone was not primarily intended to reduce unemployment, but, rather, to reduce production costs. The labor force of choice, therefore, was abundant but located at some distance from the sphere of productive economic activity. Young women represented, as they did during the nineteenth century, a great discovery for capital. In 1979, in the underdeveloped countries, some one million women worked in export assembly operations. This represented half of the total number of women working in industrial manufacturing (Carrillo and Hernández 1982: 24).

Mexico's maquiladora labor force is approximately 80 percent female (SPP 1980). Female labor is abundant in the underdeveloped countries, cheaper than its male counterpart, and endowed with social attributes that permit the exercise of a greater degree of control. In Mexico, as in other underdeveloped countries, the mean duration of employment is about three years, while in modern industries with advanced technology, where female labor predominates, employment duration has averaged between four and five years. Mexico's maquiladoras are also characterized by high turnover, which results as much from the abundance of labor as from demand for that labor.

The great benefit of maquiladoras to foreign investors involves the possibility of reducing production costs while expanding markets, both of which mean higher productivity. For government and private enterprise, the establishment of these plants partially resolved the problem of unemployment and thereby thwarted the political consequences that would have ensued had no measures been taken. Hence, the Mexican government sought to create the material, economic, and communications infrastructure needed to attract foreign capital. Places like Tijuana, located as they are in the designated *zona libre*, or duty-free zone, insulated from the national economy, enjoying tax-free status, and situated close to the United States, represent paradise for these transnational enterprises. They are advantageous in terms of cost and access to communications, transportation, industrial parks, and customs facilities. The combination offers local financing viability, low administrative salaries, low production-factor costs (electricity, telephone, maintenance, and labor), minimal training requirements, little regulation of labor conditions and environmental pollution, and effective exemption from federal labor law requirements. The firms can likewise count on political stability, labor discipline, and the weakness or near-absence of labor unions.

The Problematic of the Female Laborer

Female workers in the maquiladoras, like most female workers, are subject to a double workday. This characteristic makes the task of analyzing the situation of female workers more complex than analyzing that of their male counterparts. The female worker, apart from her exploitation as a worker, is oppressed as a woman:

> for men and women alike, exploitation has to do with the economic reality of capitalist class relations, whereas oppression refers to women and minorities as they are situated within the structure of patriarchal, racial, and capitalist relations. Exploitation is what male and female workers experience in the labor force. The oppression of women proceeds from their exploitation as salaried workers; it is compounded by those relations that determine women's existence within a patriarchal and sexual hierarchy as both domestic workers and consumers. Racial oppression—the enforcement of the society's racial divisions—compounds the effects of economic exploitation, making the reality of minority women even more complex. Power—or its inverse, oppression—derives from sex, race, and class, all of which manifest through the material and ideological dimensions of patriarchy, racism, and capitalist relations of production. Oppression reflects the hierarchical relations of sexual and racial divisions at work and within the larger society. (Eisenstein 1980: 34)

Patriarchal relations inhibit the development of human potential. As long as these patriarchal relations exist, the perception and experience of life are quite different for women and men. The sexual division of labor and the division of labor in society at large determine people's activities, their worldview, their desires, and their aspirations. Patriarchy divides men and women and consigns each of them to their respective roles within a gender hierarchy while structuring their obligations in relation to the distinctive domain of the family, and within the political economy (Eisenstein 1980: 34).

The role of women within the capitalist system is to physically and socially reproduce the workforce, whether working in or outside of the home—that is to say, to produce men and women capable of serving as a productive labor force. In this manner, female maquiladora workers engage in production, reproduction, and consumption.

Yet it is apparent that the socialization involved in the work experience favors a widening of female horizons previously focused on the routine problems of the family. The social experience of work facilitates the possibility that the feminine condition no longer assumes the appearance of being

> an inevitable consequence of an inhumane form of social organization that transforms men into machines of production . . . [and women] into the "attendants" of those machines. As part of the social organization of capitalist production, women have discovered who has been responsible for their oppression, and whose interests have truly been served by their domestic slavery. This is a lesson that cannot be forgotten. (Broyelle 1975: 78)

Hence, all the women represented here were disposed, and perhaps felt it necessary, to speak, to relate what it means to be a worker, a mother, a partner, a migrant, and a woman. All had something in common, and all had assimilated the fundamental vocabulary of industrial workers: enter, leave, move, haul, tighten, pull the lever, push the button, produce, don't smoke or chat on the job, don't get tired. And still, they never forgot the "magic" words of womanhood: buy, cook, sweep, iron, care for the children, don't sit down, educate, make love, go away, shut up. Because of all this, their speech assumes definition, purpose, and meaning.

Beautiful Flowers of the Maquiladora

1.

Meeting the Demand

"Listen up, girls! We need your cooperation. We have an order to fill, and we're going to schedule several shifts. The only way to increase production is to change some of you to other shifts. Those of you who have been with us the longest will have to work with the new girls to accelerate the pace and meet the quota."

Ángela commented with annoyance:

You have to make the supervisors understand your situation, because some of us have children and others have to cater to their husbands. Everybody has her own concerns! Anyway, what happens is, there are many of us older women in the factory and the supervisors want us all to quit.[1] The bosses insist on changing our shifts; there's just no other way. They do it to wear us down and make us quit on our own, so they won't have to pay severance.

She paused, searching for words:

Same old story! One time they assigned a bunch of us to night shift for five months. At last we were able to speak with the manager, and he put us back on our regular shift. I was the one who spoke up!

Her face spread with a smile at the memory, and after shifting in the kitchen chair, she sat back to continue her account:

The manager said he had no idea that those of us on night shift were the old-timers, those to whom he owes so much. Not for nothing have we been such good workers. He was a nice American who told us that if we had a contract to work a specified shift, no one had the right to change us to another one.

Before he told us all this, we tried every day to see him in order to speak with him. Some twenty or thirty of us went, and I was the leader. Although I don't know how to express myself very well, they all said that I should be the one to speak. They pushed me up front and I had to speak with him. The doorman always told us that the manager was out. Pure lies! We tried eight days in a row, and finally one day I made myself do it. I spoke with the manager just as he was leaving for his house on the other side. "Oh, sir," I said to him, "all of us girls are working the night shift, even though we've already been working here for quite some time on the morning shift."

"Let's see, Angelita, call Socorro over here," he replied. This woman is the boss of the whole plant [the plant supervisor]. It terrified me just thinking that I had to call her to speak with the American. Walking over to her, I was sure they were going to fire me. How could it be that I, a mere operator, was going to tell the plant supervisor that the manager wanted to see her? I thought they were going to fire me, but I thought that if they did, they would give me all my money [severance pay]. That calmed me down. When we got to where the girls were standing with the manager, Socorro became very nervous, and her face turned red.

The manager addressed her, "These ladies are old hands and they have their regular shift, but you have them working from ten at night until six in the morning! What's the deal? You know they have their specified hours and that they can't be switched just like that to another shift. How can you do that to people who have been working with us for so long?" Speaking in an energetic voice to Socorro, the manager continued, "Effective tomorrow, all you women will have your normal shift back, I promise you."

Angelita paused for a breath: "Really, thank God he switched us back, because it was a killer to work all night and get home just in time to make breakfast and clean the house, before trying to get some sleep with all the daytime racket."

Ángela was grateful to the manager. She associated the North American with the good and the humane. At various times she has commented to me that they should replace all the Mexican supervisors[2] with North Americans, because the latter are much better. Many female factory workers shared this notion. In their opinion, the Mexicans were tyrants, good-for-nothings. The women concurred in viewing the North Americans as more responsible, more considerate, and, above all, more appreciative and considerate of women. As one observed, "We have never had North American supervisors, but I know that they're better because those who have been to the factory, the engineers and the coordinators, are very nice people."

The workers at Ángela's plant once proposed to the manager that he replace all the Mexican supervisors with North Americans. He smiled at the flattery of his North American pride. "Let's see what we can do," he responded, but nothing changed. Clearly, the firm has no interest in changing supervisors. It is necessary to maintain the reputation of the considerate North American, but the supervisor, as an intermediary representing the owners' interests, can rarely afford to be considerate. Besides, a North American supervisor would earn a very high salary, paid in dollars. Such an arrangement would let the workers see that their difficulties are not a question of nationality, but one of the fundamental organization of labor. Their situation is the result of a prevailing model of productive organization in which manual labor is the key element.

Ángela was quite nervous, shifting from foot to foot as she spoke. It was as though her years of assembling cassettes had left their mark on the rhythm of her life:

> Normally I get up at five in the morning. I get dressed, make the bed, have coffee or a smoothie for breakfast, and leave with six of my co-workers in Margarita's car. She charges us for gas and a bit more for the service. As soon as we arrive we punch in and put on the smock the company gave us to wear when we were hired, which we have to wash and mend ourselves. We clean the machines and we cover our legs with plastic because it's so cold. The roof is tin, so when it's cold we have to wear a sweater and overcoat, and when it's hot, it's like an oven.
>
> In the factory I've had two separate jobs. The first was to assemble the cassettes, to put everything inside the little case. They give us the insides and we have to assemble them. You sit in front of the machine, open the cassette, and separate the two sides. Then with a little tool we put small pieces of plastic in each base. We have a large roll of recording tape on a base that spins, controlled by two buttons that thread and wind the tape. These become the little rolls of recording tape inside the cassettes. The rolls can be of 30, 40, 45, 60, 90, or 110 minutes.
>
> Winding the tape goes very quickly, a question of seconds. As soon as it's wound, the machine stops, and in that time you should have prepared the cassette, which has tin, rolls, negatives, boards, and cotton. The time it takes the machine to wind the tape varies according to the size of the cassette. If it's 30 minutes, it hardly takes any time at all, and there's not enough time to prepare the cassette. For 60-minute cassettes and longer, it's possible, but you

have to do it very rapidly because, as I already mentioned, it's a question of seconds. When the machine stops, you push a button to cut the tape. Then you take the little roll and start assembling another one immediately. You close the cassette and put it in the out box and start preparing another cassette, which winds in 5 seconds. I make the entire cassette, putting them in boxes of 100, very carefully, because they are still not glued or screwed together yet and they can come apart.

Each line of workers—only women work in this plant—has a belt that conveys the full box to the press, where a number of women either glue or screw the cassettes together. On each full box they put a note with a number that tells them who assembled the cassettes, and if any of them are faulty, they reject them and we have to do them over again. The work is very monotonous! I could do over 800 cassettes a day, although the number varied according to which size cassette I had to assemble on any given day.

Angelita worked ten hours a day except Fridays, when she happily left two hours earlier, for a total of forty-eight hours of work a week. She often made more than eight hundred cassettes a day. It would be impressive to see her complete the necessary steps in only one minute and twenty seconds. These are fleeting movements, the prestidigitation of a magician, recalling the familiar adage that the hand is quicker than the eye. Ángela continued:

Some cassettes require lubrication, and those take longer because you have to use a little tool to apply a bit of grease. It also depends on the grade or quality of the cassette. In some cases, the tape has to be shiny on one side and dull on the other; if the tape is a little bit folded or creased, it won't thread, and that slows you down more. Other kinds of tape are less delicate, which makes their assembly much easier; we can make many more cassettes under those circumstances. At times they ask each of us assemblers to make a thousand cassettes with the fine tape, and we meet the quota, but we have to work extra hours. At such times we earn more money but we exhaust ourselves. Now, since the first devaluation of 1976, we've begun to be paid in pesos, and it no longer makes sense to work the extra hours for so little money. Anyway, we're a lot more tired now.

I lasted seven years assembling cassettes, and I was doing the same thing for hours, days, and years. I got so tired that I asked for a transfer. I was so exhausted that I felt like my lungs were collaps-

ing. At times I arrived home crying from the pain. I went to a
private doctor and he told me I was very tired, that the best thing
would be to rest a bit, although he knew that I couldn't stop
working. He said that if I continued working, my lungs were going
to collapse. They ignored my complaints at Social Security.[3] They
said there was nothing wrong with me, and they sent me back
home without doing anything. They never even took an X ray to
see what was going on with me.

At that point I could no longer assemble cassettes. I could hardly
do anything, which bothered me because before I had been the
quickest, the one who produced the most. Each day I did less, until
I spoke with the supervisor, who told me she couldn't do anything,
that I should speak with the production chief.[4] He told me he
would do everything possible to shift me, and that if the packing
chief agreed, they would send me over there. He arranged everything, and the next day they sent me to that department.

I felt that in making cassettes I had sacrificed my life, as if in
that seat and in that work station I had left behind something of
my being. I felt like a new person in the new post. I experienced
the nervousness of the person who begins a new job, who wants to
fit in with the rest, and with oneself. At first I had no time to think
of anything but the work. A different task always requires a lot of
concentration. Little by little I gained skill, and now I've got it
down. That's where I've been ever since.

When I was assembling cassettes, I could think of good and
bad things. If my workmates were not chatting with me I could
reflect on my life for hours at a time, my daughter and many
other things. . . . But turning the same thing over in your mind
again and again is no good! At times I thought of my past life,
and I was anguished over not having all my children with me. I
thought, or rather I dreamed, that perhaps I might be able to give
the best to my children so that they wouldn't have to experience
what I've been through, so they might study and be decent, upright
individuals.

For Angelita, reflecting on the past was a kind of masochism. She was
plagued by the memory of her children who were not with her and the
anguish of solitude. At a very young age she married a man who
frequently beat her. After a number of separations she decided to leave
Comala, Colima, with her three children. The day she left, her husband
surprised her and took away the two younger ones. He didn't let them see
her for many years. "He took away my daughter, who was only ten
months old." Angelita went to Tepic with her eldest daughter, and, later,

looking for better opportunities, she went to Tijuana to work in the maquiladoras. She continued:

In the factory's good times we were sixteen hundred women making cassettes. There was a lot of competition among us, and none of us wanted to let up. We ate in ten minutes instead of the fifty minutes the company allowed, because we were interested in making more cassettes than our counterparts. I had a very good record; they took all the women on our line out to eat a number of times as a prize for having been the most productive group. During that period I never felt any aches and pains, and I didn't feel exhausted. Initially, I earned $18.99 a week, then $26.50, $36.00, and $56.00. Then, after the devaluation, we began to be paid in pesos. We were all very angry because we preferred to be paid in dollars, but the company said it was not convenient.

I have always cooperated with the bosses and managers of the factory. I always worked extra hours and produced a lot. I can't do that any longer, and they can't force me. And although they ask me to work extra hours, I don't do it anymore, now that I cannot; I feel tired out. I need the extra money from overtime, but I need my health more.

Now I'm in the packing department. I pack the cassettes that have already been labeled according to the buyer's requirements. The firm that places the order sends the plastic mix used to make the cassette: the label, the bag (if they want it bagged), or the little box if they want it packed. They also send the card stock that they put in the cassette boxes, where they write the names of the songs they are going to record. The cassette leaves the plant ready to be sold.

At the moment, my job consists of handling the card stock on which they write the names of the songs they record. I handle thousands and thousands of pieces of card stock daily. I do up to ninety-five or one hundred boxes of 260 cassettes. That is, I pack some twenty-five thousand or twenty-six thousand little boxes a day. I get bored, I get annoyed, I curse. I take a trip to the bathroom.

Sometime "Okis" [other trained workers] and the supervisor help me. Yesterday, for example, they put me on a task that I don't do. They assigned me to put cassettes in the cases. I don't know how to do that the way it's supposed to be done. I don't have any experience. The supervisor put me on it because I refused to switch from day to night shift for a few days. She assigned me the job as a form of punishment. I work very slowly, and although you can control the speed of the machine, I stopped it because I couldn't keep up. The supervisor knew we wouldn't make the production goal because I was working slowly, and this order was a rush job. But she wanted to punish me, so she put me with a woman who works very fast. And every time I turned off the machine, she turned it back on. She gave me a rough time, but God is great: He tightens the grip but doesn't strangle you. We made the quota. . . . We did eighty-six boxes of 260 cassettes—on the first day!

The supervisor said to me, "So you can't do it, eh?"

Yes," I replied, "but ask me how I feel. My back is giving out; it feels like I'm going to collapse!"

What is important to them is meeting the quota. Yesterday a number of *muchachas* had to work from four in the afternoon until two in the morning. Fortunately, in four days I'm going to return to my machine putting card stock in the cassette cases.

The work can appear easy, especially if one observes Ángela in action. Her movements are exact; there is no confusion in their order. Her quickness makes the work look simple, relaxed. The machines seem to move slowly, as do the conveyor belts. But attempting to equal the speed with which Angelita executes the tasks is enough to make one realize just how painstaking, monotonous, and wearisome the work actually is. "Work, the sole contemporary god, has done away with creation. Infinite work without end signifies a life without purpose in modern society" (Paz 1982: 182).

Ángela considered herself old for this type of work, and, practically speaking, she had limited work opportunities. This obliged her to keep her thoughts to herself and keep on working, but what she really wanted was to quit working altogether.

I have to work rapidly despite perspiration and back pain. If I don't work rapidly, I don't meet the quota; then I get nervous and they get on me. There is no feeling more desperate than seeing the pieces accumulate while your companions go on working. On various occasions I've had the urge to cry, scream, to leave every-thing and run out, to start some other job and to stop doing the same old thing. But at forty-two years of age it is very difficult to secure another job. In Tijuana there are few work opportunities for women, especially for us older women who have only a primary school education. In the shops and factories they prefer young girls, especially in the shops, where they choose only pretty, well-dressed young girls.

I could do piecework at home, but that is a hard job and they don't pay well. Besides, then you don't have Social Security. So I will keep on making cassettes and controlling my nerves in order to keep my present job.

Almost none of the tasks Ángela and the other female maquiladora workers perform involve any development of intellectual or creative capacity. They require only conforming to a repetitive process like that described by Charlie Chaplin in *Modern Times*: tighten a particular type of screw a thousand and one times. This repetitive activity limits creativity and thus is little valued. Nonetheless, the worker, as a potentially creative human being, even in the monotony of her labor, succeeds in making technological innovations. Working causes her to become a disciplined being and to systematize her life according to a strict schedule of clocking in, leaving, eating, resting. She must adapt herself to a way of life regimented by the firm. Of course, this is not something exclusive to the maquiladora; such regimentation extends to all workers, including bureaucrats, and it is considered a requisite function in any enterprise.

Repetitive and monotonous jobs performed principally by female maquiladora workers range from dressing dolls to sewing collars on shirts, counting grocery coupons, assembling toys, preparing chemical compounds, and soldering sophisticated electronics equipment.

Elena, a pleasant twenty-five-year-old, addressed me:

Look, every kind of factory job is a pain, and I'm speaking from experience. Most of us girls work from necessity, some to get out of the house and earn a little money for this and that, but I doubt that any do it for entertainment or because work enchants them. No way, girl, only in the movies! Listen to me. One time I was working in a factory where we made dolls out of rags, and with plastic heads. The dolls had the head of that famous little pig you see on TV [Miss Piggy, the Muppet character popularized in the U.S. mass media]. It was a factory where they only made dolls. I had to dress the dolls as they went by on a conveyor belt that ran really fast. I had to grab them, dress them, and put them back on the belt. I forget the number of dolls I dressed in a day, but I know it was thousands, so many that at various times I dreamed that Miss Piggy was attacking and killing me.

I had to pull their little clothes on from the neck down and fasten two tiny buttons. For sure, these little dolls say good-bye and hello, but nothing in the world would make me buy one of the dolls for myself or my daughter. I hate them.

We never had a fixed production standard; we just had to make as many dolls as the supervisor wanted, the number demanded by the buyer. All of us girls stood in a kind of circle, and as the conveyor belt went by, some of us grabbed the dolls to dress them, and the rest did other things to the dolls. The pace was so swift that very quickly the dolls began to stack up. When that happened the supervisor would come to reprimand us, and we just got more agitated.

The work was unpleasant. My hands really ached, every day worked to the bone by the speed of the work. My hands hurt so much that when I got home I couldn't do the housework; I couldn't even change my son's diapers.

One day I just couldn't go on, and I told the supervisor that I wasn't going to work anymore, that my hands just couldn't take it. "No," he said, "wait until quitting time. Don't you see that the dolls are going to stack up on your co-workers?" I answered, "Who cares?" In any case, I tried to continue working, but I went very slowly, because my hands hurt so much. They couldn't take any more. Then the old man came up to me and asked, "Why do you have so many dolls stacked up?" I replied, "I just can't do the work." He told me, "Well, just quit then." "That's what I'm going to do. I was just waiting for you in order to submit my resignation." Angrily, I left the dolls there and walked out. I lasted only one month.

Elena had worked at five maquiladoras, and she always ended up quitting because she found the work extremely tiring and detrimental to her health. She was quite active and critical, always moving about and reflecting on this or that; in short, she was a bundle of nerves. In contrast, Ángela was cautious; she nurtured the hope that one day she would marry a good and responsible man who would rescue her from having to work so that she could dedicate herself to her four children and her home.

Elena confirmed that she had been able to leave the maquiladora because she had a husband whose job as a taxi driver was sufficient to support them both without her having to work. But Ángela could not even consider leaving the maquiladora because "her husband left her" fourteen years earlier. Since that time she had worked in order to support her children and help them "get ahead." By this she meant ensuring that they are well nourished and that they get an education, "so they don't have to be laborers" like her.

Gabriela's case was quite distinct from Ángela's and Elena's. Gabriela was a young single woman, twenty-six years of age. At her plant she was known as quick and hard-working. Like Elena and Ángela, she was a

migrant who came to Tijuana in search of employment. Gabriela
reflected on the years she had dedicated to work in various capacities at
the same maquiladora:

> The third day I was in Tijuana, a girlfriend took me to look for
> work. In the first factory I went to, they were looking for workers
> and they quickly handed me an application. I remember that the
> manager came out of his office and asked me where I was from and
> how old I was. I told him the truth, that I had recently turned
> fifteen and that I had just arrived from Acaponeta. He told me he
> was going to take me on, even though I was still rather young to
> work. He filled in my application and told me that I should send a
> request to my hometown for my primary school diploma and my
> birth certificate. Several times he told me that if anyone asked me
> my age, I was to tell them that I was sixteen. If not, he said, he
> would have problems, and so would I.
>
> I was quite nervous. I was afraid that I wouldn't be able to do
> what they would ask of me. The manager took me to the supervi-
> sor, and she showed me what I was going to do. It was an electron-
> ics factory where we made airplane parts, very complicated equip-
> ment. I was one of three hundred workers, only twelve of whom
> were men. I began working in the department that did the final
> testing of rectifiers; my job was to test these things called diodes. I
> had to test their voltage and classify them, a job I did for close to
> three years. Then they moved me to the screw department, where I
> had to mark them according to size and the job for which they
> were intended.
>
> On various occasions I also had to make the three types of
> screws produced at the factory. They were made in molds, and
> each mold required a distinct soldering technique. By that time I
> already knew how to do nearly all the tasks at each station, be-
> cause they moved us around so we could learn to do everything on
> those days when one of the *muchachas* might be absent. For a long
> time we would perform five or six different jobs in a single day. On
> those days I didn't get bored because everything was new. Later,
> they moved me to the rectifier assembly area, where I had to set up
> the unit and send it on to be soldered. This was assembly line
> work, but, fortunately, it ran very slowly, and we rarely were
> pressed because we worked at an easy rhythm.
>
> I was on that job for a year and seven months, then they moved
> me to the chemical room. In that department I had to make chemi-
> cal mixtures, and it was quite dangerous because we did not have

all the necessary laboratory safety and ventilation equipment. I worked with a variety of acids: nitric, sulfuric, hydrofluoric, acetic. We also worked with trichloroethylene, acetone, nickel, freon, and other substances. I breathed those acid vapors for many hours on end; often ventilation was poor, and I would get sick to my stomach. One time they had to put me on worker's compensation for four months because my body was completely saturated with the chemicals. I received various detoxification treatments at the Social Security clinic, and they told me I could no longer work with chemicals. My stomach burned a great deal and I had constant headaches. When I returned to the job, I went to work again in the chemicals room; I felt like I was going to faint, and I began to feel ill again. So I requested a transfer to another department.

The room still lacks good fans, and the ones they have often don't work at all. I don't know how the *muchachas* keep working there, because neither the general conditions nor the safety measures have been improved in the least. Surely, they are going to suffer the same problems that I did. That work with acids is very exacting and dangerous, because if you don't mix the chemicals properly, they can explode. Everything has to be done by the book, using precise measures. Despite the hazardous nature of the work, and the fact that you must be specially trained to do it, they pay the same as for any other job, and they fail to recognize its critical importance.

One time there was an explosion and two co-workers were burned. Fortunately, their clothing was stripped off right away and they were washed down, which kept them from being badly burned. If the chemicals had gotten on them, even one drop in the eyes, they would have been blinded. One of the safety measures that we did have was goggles, but we rarely used them because they made us so hot, as the room has no ventilation.

I was transferred to the packing department. I had to mark every product with the date and production number. I lasted only a year at that job because it was so dull and tiring. You had to really concentrate to avoid mistakes. If I made a mistake, it required seven people to correct the error. They had to erase the labels before they dried and return them to be numbered again.

After that I became a mechanic in the department where they solder under a microscope. I was able to become a mechanic because the managers decided to train various people in the factory for the better-compensated and more prestigious position of mechanic. Around twenty-three of us enrolled. We took the courses and gained experience, but they gave jobs to only three of us, the ones who did well on the tests and whose personality was judged best suited to the job. Of the three mechanics, I am the only woman. Now when I arrive at the factory I punch in, put on my smock, open the nitrogen and water valves on the machines, and turn them on, along with the air conditioning.

It's very important to check that the water and nitrogen valves are open, because otherwise the machines will burn out. After that, I check my tools and get to work. I fix all the machines that are out of order. At times, when I haven't been able to fix something, I try to improvise, and if that fails, I seek help from another technician, and we rack our brains to come up with a solution.

At times, I get so exhausted from pondering how to fix something that I have to step outside for some air in order to be able to continue my job. The work is never monotonous, but it has its hazards, because I can get electrocuted by a machine if I forget to disconnect it before starting repairs. I could even get killed if I forget.

When I work I can think only about work. I have to concentrate. But when I'm not involved with repairs, I'm quite relaxed and can think about other things.

There is competition among the mechanics, but we almost always help one another. The tools we work with are quite old, leftovers from other departments. We don't always have what we need and have to go to other departments to borrow what we need, or just grab a tool from somewhere in order to be able to work. That's how we collected the tools we need, and we are very careful about keeping track of them. Every month we take inventory of all the tools in the plant, because otherwise we have nothing to work with.

The mechanic's work is anything but boring because you are always doing something new and learning in the process. To be a mechanic you need a certain kind of personality because you deal directly with many kinds of people. You have to know what's what, otherwise your co-workers will jerk you around. For example, the workers say their machine is out of order, but the truth is, it's fine. What they want is just to rest for a moment.

I deal with a lot of different types; we number some sixty in my department, with only six men. For me it's a lot easier to work with men than with women because with women there are more arguments and disputes. My position in the factory has created problems for me because I don't have a supervisor, and the fact that I have no one who directs or orders me around makes other

The heat and strong chemical odors make the work harder and more risky.

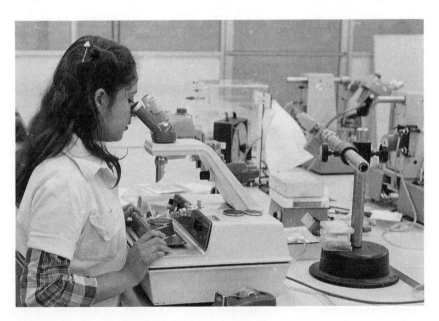

Delicate jobs require precision and patience.

Long working hours strain the eyes, as the women solder small parts with the aid of a microscope.

workers envious. It seems like you can't have everything in life. Now I earn more and my work is interesting, but I've earned the envy of a lot of people.

Gabriela enjoyed a privileged position among the workers at her plant. Her work was creative and was better compensated. But few have this possibility, and few escape the tyranny imposed by production quotas, badgering by their supervisors, and the numbing tedium of the work.

Personnel policies vary from factory to factory and also depend on the department in which one works. In the plant where Gabriela worked, very few women had been promoted to more specialized positions. The owners' interest in training is entirely pragmatic: only a handful of laborers gain competency in all aspects of the operation, and only so that they can substitute in case of absences that might otherwise slow daily production.

Because production takes top priority, management seeks ways to raise it; manipulating the quota is an excellent means to that end. The quota ostensibly represents the total hourly output that a worker is capable of producing. It constitutes a legal means of exploiting workers, because the federal labor statute prohibits both the extension of the workday and the reduction of salaries.

The quotas serve to extract maximum productivity from the workers. Many of the maquiladoras have industrial engineering departments in which technicians carry out time-and-motion studies to determine standards for each task and each production line.[5]

There is an essential difference between U.S. production standards, which are seen as aims to be met, and Mexican standards, which are seen as the minimum necessary for every worker to meet in order to keep his or her job. Industrial engineering utilizes two fundamental methods to determine the standard of production. MTM (movement-time measurement) derives a standard for the output of a "normal" operator in a "normal" time interval; the work factor relies on a system of incentives to motivate the worker to produce the maximum. A less-sophisticated method involves the use of the stopwatch.

The first two methods are the more precise and greatly reduce the percentage of error in measuring a worker's execution of a task. These methods are supported by an ample body of scientific research, principally achieved through the use of cameras with variable-speed motors that enable complicated filming techniques. The technician applying these methods requires no special proficiency in camera or film technology. It is sufficient to consult standardized tables developed for each method or a measuring tape to gauge short distances. Each method relies on a series of tables that classify diverse types of body movement (arm, forearm, hand, finger, leg, and foot). These tables also take into consideration the intention of each movement (lifting, positioning, exerting pressure, weighing, shifting sight lines) with respect to the object being manipulated. Based on these factors, each component movement is assigned a set duration, expressed in seconds, which determines the time allotted to the entire job.

Despite this body of research, many maquiladoras use none of these methods. Production standards based on the exigencies of production are arbitrarily imposed. They are also used as a means to increase competition between workers.

The coercive nature of the production standards, together with the worker's desire to save time, motivate the women to find ways to work faster. In this way they come up with practical innovations that the firm is quick to appropriate and apply to production. But firms neither compensate nor acknowledge these innovations as coming from the workers. Gabriela commented:

> If it weren't for the way that we all invent ways to increase production, the orders would never be met. One time a co-worker quit, and they forced me to do her work as well as my own. I might have been able to do it, and if not, I would have looked for a way. But I

didn't do it because they don't pay me for it. Besides, if I do it once just because I'm a good person, the next time they demand it; they come to expect it of me.

Alma, a woman of forty-two from Oaxaca, remarked with a trace of nostalgia and pride:

I quit because I was fed up and exhausted. No woman in the maquiladora stands up for her rights, neither here nor on the other side of the border. That's why the owners prefer to hire women.

Alma had just left the maquiladora where she had been involved in a struggle to organize female workers:

I had been working for six years in a textile maquiladora, where I nearly destroyed my kidneys and my eyes. I never earned a fixed salary. They paid me by the job, on a piecework basis, as they also call it. In this maquiladora here, we work quite differently from the way they do in other textile plants.

We women did the complete piece. They gave each of us a pattern, and we had to make the dress nearly from beginning to end. They gave us the cut material and we had to sew it together. It wasn't like the majority of textile maquiladoras, where the work is very segmented. That is, some sew the sleeves, others the collar, others put on the buttons, zippers, and so forth. By contrast, here they are always changing the pattern according to variations in fashion and changing seasons. We just about get used to making something and gain some skill with a piece, then they change it on us!

The dresses we make are beautiful, for very fashionable women. They're incredibly expensive! They sell them in the best stores in the United States and they cost $200 or $300. And what do we get? We make 45 pesos [about U.S.$1.00] per dress. Incredible, don't you think? We spend ten hours a day in front of a sewing machine to make a man rich and we don't even know him. And the worst of it is that we continue doing it, some not even making the minimum wage, without complaining, asleep at the wheel, watching time go by, years in front of the sewing machine. I recognize the glares, I know how we protest on the inside because we don't dare say anything to the bosses. We wait for the quitting bell to ring so we can hit the street, believing that it's all a bad dream, and that it's going to change. It's like we put these thoughts aside for a moment and go back to work, without doing anything more about it. At times we forget why the devil we're working, just waiting for a little bit of money so our kids can survive.

You get used to it all, or at least we pretend to. At times we let ourselves be carried away by the noise or the music of the radios we all carry. It helps us forget the fatigue and the back pain we all have from working in front of the sewing machine. The moment came when I just couldn't take any more and I quit, knowing that the money my husband makes, together with what our oldest daughter gives us, wasn't going to be enough. I knew we were in for some hard times, but I never knew just how much. Nobody anticipated these two currency devaluations, the one in February and the one in August [1982]. Now everything is priced out of sight, and I have to hustle to find another job, because every day things just get worse.

The good thing is that in the sewing factories they don't want only the youngest women, like in the electronics plants. The bosses here want talented seamstresses with a lot of experience, and that's all I've ever done in my life. At times I dream about how my life might be different somehow.

Elena, Gabriela, and Alma were quite aware of how low their salaries were with respect to the physical toll extracted by their work. In plain terms, these women pinpointed why maquiladora operations have invested in Mexico, as they have in other underdeveloped nations: salaries are much lower than they are in industrialized countries, and they have a large number of people who will work for very low wages.

For the workers in Alma's sewing factory, the disparity between the real costs of production and the actual selling prices of the products was obvious. These women could easily see that profit derives in no small part from the unremunerated labor they performed. They were aware of the huge and growing economic surplus produced by maquiladoras. These plants produce sophisticated equipment used in the manufacture of computers, airplanes, missiles, and so forth. These products—microcircuits and rectifiers, among others—are not goods commonly used by the population at large. They are not products that appear in the shop windows, or whose market value is commonly known among the general public. Moreover, in most cases, the worker herself does not even know what it is that she actually produces, much less what its market price is. Ignorance of the product's use and of its value prevents the worker from perceiving the process by which merchandise accrues value. This poses obstacles to the workers' becoming conscious of the direct linkage that exists between their labor and the creation of surplus value.[6]

The large firms that build maquiladoras along Mexico's northern frontier also have subsidiaries in other underdeveloped countries, as well as in the United States, where their headquarters generally are located. Workers in the maquiladoras of northern Mexico cannot find out for whom they work, the use of the product they manufacture, or the value it might have. These conditions have grave implications for efforts to organize labor and raise worker consciousness. The situation recalls nineteenth-century accounts of English laborers smashing the machines that they held responsible for their exploitation. Workers' ignorance of what they produce and for whom they labor severely impedes their potential for organization and leaves them little leverage with which to negotiate.

Notes

1. The Federal Labor Law requires severance pay equal to three months' salary plus twenty days' salary for each year worked. Severance pay need not be paid if the worker quits. Thus, if a business wants to get rid of an employee, that employee may be pressured to quit.

2. Even though technically the plant manager is over the supervisor, the supervisor actually has much more power over individual workers. He is the one who has more direct and daily contact with the workers and can influence the manager for or against individual employees. Therefore the workers fear the plant supervisor much more than the manager, who is often North American and has only tangential contact with them. It is the supervisor who poses much more of a threat to their employment and whom they fear more for the control he has over their lives.

3. Instituto Mexicano del Seguro Social (IMSS) is the Mexican national public health system.

4. Although not true for all plants, the following is a typical example of the plant management hierarchy: at the top is the plant manager or general manager, then the section managers, followed by the superintendents or production chiefs, after which come the supervisors, the assembly line managers, and, finally, the workers. Within the labor force itself there are also various categories, which differ from plant to plant.

5. This information was obtained in interviews with production managers and technicians at electronics plants in Ciudad Juárez and Tijuana between 1979 and 1982. Braverman (1975), Coriat (1979), and Linhart (1979) were useful in carrying out the analysis. A recent analytical work on industrial engineering theory is Neffa (1990).

6. The analysis offered here is informed by a reading of Amin (1977), Bagu et al. (1983), Mandel (1978), Marini (1974, 1983), and Poulantzas (1976).

2.

The Realm of Work

Maquiladora plants conceal enigmas that cannot always be detected at first glance. The factories are nondescript; the low, dilapidated buildings do not stand out from the rest of the cityscape. But merely to enter is inevitably to be struck by four conditions that invite reflection on the plants' injurious effects on worker health: the penetrating odor produced by the caustic blend of chemical fumes and vaporized solder; the infernal din of the machines combined with the music of the radios that every worker carries or the Muzak piped in by the firm to raise production; the swirling haze of smoke, fumes, and lint that turns everything gray; and the sea of green, blue, and yellow workers' smocks, worn to protect the raw materials and to avoid contaminating the product, which must be immaculate in order to pass quality control. Elena commented:

> I was very apprehensive about going to work in a maquiladora. I preferred to find work as a domestic. I always thought that the plants could easily catch fire, because they're full of electric wires, machines, and other things. Still, I decided to go to work there because I needed the money.
>
> At first when I arrived in Tijuana, the girls I knew told me about the maquiladoras and they urged me to go to work with them. They told me, "Here they pay you every week, you get health benefits, and you know lots of people; it's not like domestic work!" I had never been inside a factory, but I had an idea of what they were like, because I had seen some in the movies and on television.
>
> The picture I had about the maquiladoras was pretty close to reality. When I went inside, I saw that the place was pretty old. It was like a refurbished warehouse with a tin roof. Oh, the dreams I have of that cursed tin roof. It's wretched! Here in Tijuana the climate is very extreme, so in winter the factory is freezing, and in summer it's an inferno.

Gabriela added:

> The plants don't have any windows. It's just walls on all sides, so
> the lights and ventilation are artificial. In winter it gets dark very
> early, so we enter and leave work in darkness; we go for days
> without seeing the sun. It's like another world. I know that work-
> ing for so many hours under artificial light is bad for the eyes, most
> of all because the lights are so poor. At times everything looks
> yellow because the light is so low. It really irritates me! What
> would it cost them to put in some more lights? I don't get it. In the
> factory where my sister works everything is very clean and well lit.
> It's a new factory, really big, with a very nice atmosphere. What we
> would give to have such a nice place to work. If one is obliged to
> work, at least it could be nice and clean, with the best conditions.
>
> Where I work, there's only one fan for the entire department of
> sixty workers. The environment is oppressive from bad ventilation;
> the air is full of gas from arsenic and other chemicals whose names
> I don't know, because we just distinguish them by the color keys
> they come marked with.
>
> The factory is in a single building divided into three depart-
> ments that are separated only by drywall partitions that don't
> reach the ceiling. The odors mix from all quarters, so that even
> though the kitchen is located at the very back of the building, in
> our department, the farthest away, we smell what's cooking. The
> odor of garlic and onions cooking always reaches us, and just as
> surely, the cooks can smell the acids and gases that we work with.
>
> Our eating area is very shoddy, several faded tables and some
> grills to warm our lunches. Next to the eating area is the casting
> department, which is the most hazardous because they use very
> toxic substances; it's always hazy there from all the gases.

The variety of productive activities within the maquiladoras and
marked differences in the degree of capital investment create considerable disparities between plants in terms of infrastructure and working
conditions. The scale ranges from enormous plants with large numbers
of employees to small firms whose grim labor conditions resemble those
of the artisan workshops of the Middle Ages.

In one of the smaller plants I got to know María Luisa, a woman of
thirty-one who was eager to talk about her experiences. Her eyes
followed me from the moment I entered the factory until the second
work break, when she stepped outside to buy something to eat from a
vendor's cart. As she basked in the light of day, enjoying her bean burrito
and a Coca-Cola, I remarked that I'd like to know more about her work.

After chatting for five minutes, she gave me her address so that I might visit her there and we might converse away from prying ears and free of the pressures of work: "What I can tell you, any of the women who work in the industry might tell you just as well, but I have worked in eight different plants, so I have a lot of things to relate." She spoke between bites, and her hands trembled a little. As soon as the factory bell sounded, she stubbed out her half-smoked cigarette and tucked it into the pocket of her smock. Turning to go back to work, she said, "I'll be waiting for you at my house on Monday, anytime after six in the evening."

María Luisa's daily quota was to solder one thousand resistors. Like some of her workmates, she used gloves to protect her hands from burns:

> Now, after two years of soldering, I've learned to work while wearing the gloves the firm gives us. The majority of the girls don't use them because they're a hindrance; wearing them, they can't meet the quota the bosses expect of us. The fact is, you burn your hands even with gloves, but after seeing how black the gloves get after a week of use, I've decided to use them. Even if the bosses badger me, I prefer to wear the gloves and go more slowly rather than ruin my hands. If I did that, then I'd be good for nothing, worthless even in my own house.
>
> The same thing happens to the eyes of those unlucky women whose work requires them to solder under the microscope, straining their eyes in bad light all day long. After a couple of years those girls inevitably end up wearing glasses. They're always complaining that daylight hurts their eyes and that they get headaches nearly every day. Their eyes burn and become inflamed, and they develop blurred vision.
>
> The worst drawback of maquiladora work is all the damage we do to our health. Factory labor involves working with acids and solvents,[1] handling hot materials, and for many women, long hours of working with a microscope.
>
> In the sewing maquiladoras they also have problems. Workers always have irritated throats, they develop coughs, and many become asthmatic from the lint that comes out of the fabrics they work with. Their heads turn gray like little old ladies' from so much lint. Think about it! If that's how your head looks, what must your lungs look like? Besides, from sitting in front of the sewing machine, in no time you can hardly stand the pain in your back and kidneys.

As a consequence of the way production is organized, the majority of maquiladora workers are exposed to illnesses and risks that seem inevitable. Workplace health hazards include noise, fiber inhalation, and exposure to highly toxic solids and gases, including the contaminants associated with soldering.

The hazards of the work environment vary in impact, depending on the degree and form of exposure and the intensity of production demand. Workers also are exposed to stress and fatigue that are rarely recognized by management, and sometimes not by workers themselves. But female workers comprehend the pressures exerted by the hated production standards, and those who work on the conveyor belts and assembly lines are those who most fiercely resist this type of enforced physical ruin.

The symptoms that maquiladora workers present vary considerably, depending on the type of work they perform, the substances to which they are exposed, and the form and degree of exposure. They commonly report nausea, headache, fatigue, sneezing, and coughing; irritation, pain, and inflammation of the eyes; dryness, itching, rashes, and general skin irritation; shortness of breath; irregular menstrual cycles, irritability, and insomnia. Elena related:

One co-worker had a child with a brain tumor, and she's not the only one who has had health problems with her child. Various co-workers who have worked with acids have had children with problems. We've tried to determine whether work conditions might be the cause, but nobody gives us the time of day. Everyone tells us there's just no way to know. While there may be no proof, we all know it's because of the substances that we work with, and that really alarms us. I've read in the papers that this kind of work causes problems in the blood and the nervous system, liver disease, cancer, and birth defects. That's why I say I don't want to work in the maquiladora.

Gabriela responded:

No, Elena! It's not a matter of *wanting* to work here. I don't want to work either, and here you see me, working, working. But if I don't work, how am I going to support myself, and where am I going to get the money to feed my kids? It's not just your problem, it's the problem we all face. We all run the same risk of having an accident or getting sick. We ought to organize ourselves to struggle and do something. At the very least we should demand fire extinguishers, lab coats, safety glasses, gloves, fans, face masks, and all good quality, because we've all heard Lupe's story. They give her gloves, but as soon as they get trichloroethylene on them, they turn to gum. We all need to work, we all need this miserable salary. And so? Instead of running out, we have to demand these things, because maybe the one who takes your place when you leave will be one of your daughters, or your friend. Also, we have to demand that they do away with the production standards, because working at such a fast pace is just an accident waiting to happen.

Accidents are everyday occurrences. Mercedes, a co-worker who was a solderer, developed a rheumatic condition in her hand as a result of her occupation. The hand bothered her so much that they had to operate. Now she's disabled. Another co-worker in the department got a clot in her eye, probably because of solder vapor. Also, a guy cut off his finger on the machinery. People burn themselves with solder on a daily basis, and the majority complain constantly of back pain, especially those who are just starting out. That's the worst period. During the first days your hands ache and burn, and it seems as if the body just cannot endure. With time, however, you get used to it.

Angelita said:

You know, Gabriela, where I work we have pressured them to pay us better and to improve safety measures, but because we are not united, they ignore us. We have tried to unionize, but all we have achieved is to provoke them to pressure us to work faster.

According to factory regulations, we have only five minutes to go to the bathroom. This rule went into effect only recently. For many years we were free to go to the bathroom whenever we needed to as long as we kept up. But because most of us are old-timers and are accustomed to this autonomy, we stop whenever we need to. We take responsibility for our work, and because of that we can get up three or four times and go to the bathroom and nobody says anything to us. We can do it because we have a good production record.

Nobody is supposed to eat on the factory floor, but I have to confess that many of us do so because we get hungry before break. It's really unreasonable, because we work from 7:00 A.M. to 5:30 P.M., Monday through Friday. To arrive on time I have to get up at 5:00 A.M., and at that hour you really don't feel like eating. At 9:30 they give us ten minutes for breakfast, and half an hour for lunch at 1:00 P.M. We always get hungry between breaks, so we take food onto the shop floor, "contraband," as we say.

The supervisors are quite demanding, and if we arrive late they scold us and dock us. If we are late three times they either suspend us or let us go altogether, whatever they decide. They don't let us talk, and if they see us talking they call us on it immediately. And if they catch us away from our workstation they write us up.

One always dreads being reprimanded. When the supervisors are around, all the workers change their posture to appear to be concentrating on their work. Conversations are quickly interrupted, and the only sound is that of the machinery. If a worker is called to the office, if the supervisor indicates she wants to discuss something with the worker, or if someone encounters the supervisor in the corridor during work time, her heart skips a beat. It is well known, as Robert Linhart (1979) notes, that most factories openly maintain an effectively extralegal system of surveillance and sanctions against employees caught away from their workstations or in a hallway without a pass properly signed by a supervisor, or found wanting with respect to any given production standard. One can be dismissed over any misunderstanding, punished for a delay of seconds or an impatient word to the line boss. A thousand motives suggest themselves, but you can be sure that these things will never be forgotten by the line bosses, the supervisors, the managers, whomever.

So much anxiety and fatigue just to earn the minimum wage, whose effective buying power shrinks year by year. The constant devaluations, fluctuating exchange rates, and inflation, among other factors, diminish purchasing power and make Mexico more competitive by reducing salary levels via the monetary exchange process. Salaries do not increase with seniority, nor with higher qualifications; the only way to earn more is to accept extra hours in the form of overtime.

María Luisa reported:

In the factory where I work now, I make 2,458 pesos a week [U.S.$43.00], exactly what I made in my previous job. There I worked on contract and I had never been suspended. Then one day they dismissed me. The truth is, I wasn't very happy because they had begun to demand a lot more than I was able to produce. But I thought to myself, "Having been here for so long, if I'm going to leave, well, let them give me some money." At that time I had to go see my mother in Durango, so I asked for three days' leave. I left Friday night to take advantage of the weekend, to spend more time there. They gave me three days, so I left without any worries. When I returned, they told me I was fired because I had three unexcused absences.

I wanted them to let me go, but this was completely arbitrary, because they had given me permission to miss work. What if I had been a single woman with kids, the only breadwinner? For such injustice we would have died of hunger.

I wasn't the only one they let go. That time there were seven of us women in all, and only my girlfriend and I demanded our due compensation. The others didn't even put up a fight. They said that if they complained they wouldn't be able to work anywhere else. That's not true. Well, they're partly correct because the maquiladoras are quite demanding, and they always ask for letters of recommendation, and if you get involved in a dispute, they don't give you anything. And if you stir up a lot of trouble you get blacklisted, and you don't get hired anywhere. Then you're marked. But we have to demand the rights to which we are entitled. After working like crazy and being dismissed without any compensation, it's just not right. The truth is that a lot of us don't act as we should because we don't know our rights and we're scared of the owners. That's how they can walk all over us and no one says a thing.

Factory work has its advantages and disadvantages. You work, have money, and can live better than back in the village, even though things keep getting worse. If I had stayed there I simply wouldn't have had any paid work; my only occupation would be at home. Nor would my son be in secondary school, because they have only primary school there. I believe that I will improve my life by having come to Tijuana. Here, whatever happens, I have work and a salary, and however small it may be, it helps me in many ways.

We earn this money by the sweat of our brow. Our work is exhausting. It endangers our health and after a while it makes us feel old. But ever and always, it's work. Here in Tijuana things get worse day by day. With the currency devaluation, those of us who live on the border see little promise of getting ahead. For example, my husband has been a taxi driver for some years now. Awhile back they raised the rent on his taxi. The owner charges rent in dollars, so the devaluation has doubled my husband's taxi rent in terms of pesos—and that's the way it is with everything. Rents, clothing, and lots of other goods and services are pegged to the dollar, and the merchants set the exchange rate. This is an injustice for all of us living on the border because we're in Mexico and we earn pesos.

Everything has gone up in price, and we neither organize ourselves nor protest. The Indians of Mexico used to complain, and it wasn't possible to get away with such injustice because people knew that, even if it was only with sticks, the Indians were going

to fight and defend their rights. But now it's like we are asleep.
With impunity they devalue the money on us, and nobody says a
thing. Even people much poorer than us, like the Nicaraguans,
have struggled and won, yet there are few among us here trying to
organize the people.

With anger in her voice, Alma exclaimed:

They have us by the neck! How many maquiladora operators have
told us not to strike because the workers will just get the worst of
it? How many of the owners have told us that we need to cooperate
because they represent work for so many people? Time and again
we can see how arbitration and conciliation favor the company,
and how little regard they have for the workers' interests. And
those of us who resist are dismissed as malcontents and trouble-
makers, and the other workers repudiate us. That way there can
never be any kind of worker alliance.

The maquiladoras maintain a repressive atmosphere, so a lot of
the women don't want to hear any talk of strikes. As soon as you
voice disagreement with something, they start watching you. You
try to help your fellow workers, but they're very timid. They even
refer to themselves as *pendejas*, cowards. Imagine, if they themselves nurture such a self-concept, how will they win any respect
in the workplace? I tell them what's happening is that we've been
despised all our lives, and many of us have come to believe we're
nothing. If we so resolve among ourselves, I believe that we can
improve our situation.

One time I had just spoken with one of the girls about our
treatment in the workplace, and right away the boss knew about it.
All I tried to do was organize study groups for women who had
never finished primary school, because their general awareness is
quite limited. Some cannot even add or subtract, which indicates
the kind of barriers there are to improving workers' lives.

Those women who don't want to resist lower the morale. They
don't help achieve anything. The owners step on them, pay them a
miserable wage that doesn't begin to meet their material needs,
and the workers never protest. One time we were organizing—it
was a favorable moment to push for a raise and better benefits—
and they all knuckled under.

They're totally apathetic about everything. They have a terror of
politics. You'd think the union was about to devour them. They
resist doing anything for their own benefit, and they never reflect
on their own situation. Sometimes I think we women are just

ground down and scared to organize ourselves, afraid of being denounced as "Reds." You've already seen how we women get into criticizing those who want to defend their interests as workers. Even the accountants, who are paid at the same salary level as the machine operators, defend the interests of the bosses, tooth and nail. The owners have brainwashed them.

So many girls, perhaps the majority—and I wish I were wrong— think that in the maquiladoras they have every advantage, that everything about work is just fine. So many of them are grateful just to have a chance to work. They look right past the oppressive work conditions and the owners' abuses.

I don't deny that these factories represent an employment opportunity. My desire is not that they go somewhere else—that wouldn't resolve anything. On the contrary, it would make everything worse. For the owners, we women also represent an opportunity; we work quickly, and most never complain. At the very least, the owners should improve working conditions and workplace safety. Let them spend a few of the many dollars that we enable them to make.

The export maquiladora industry on the U.S.-Mexico frontier has specific characteristics that differentiate it from the rest of Mexico's manufacturing industries. These characteristics principally involve a reliance on labor-intensive assembly operations realized outside of the country in which the investment capital originates. The internationalization of capital is a defining modality of a trend also characterized by a fragmentation of the production process and an acceleration of its pace.

Fragmentation simplifies specific operations, allowing them to be carried out rapidly and precisely by workers without training or experience. This has facilitated the creation of a workforce whose constituents were previously not integrated into the wage-earning population: women. These women represent an abundant source of labor, cheaper than male workers, and with social attributes conducive to the exercise of greater control than in the case of male workers (Carrillo and Hernández 1982a).

The fragmentation of the production process and the reliance on a labor-intensive regime favor conditions that are characteristic of maquiladoras as a whole. Working conditions have a singular impact on the cycle of worker illness and health. As already seen, these conditions are determined by the internationalization of production and the international division of labor. The export of industrialized production processes to Mexico brought the concomitant workplace hazards of the industrialized nations. But these hazards manifest differently in countries like Mexico because of the distinctive living conditions and nutritional status of the working population and workplace environmental standards, including the implementation of hygiene and safety measures and the utilization of chemical substances.

On the other hand, interest in facilitating output reflects a transformation in the organizational structure of production. Notoriously constant supervision prevails in the maquiladoras in the form of internal regulations that dictate production quotas, warnings, and quality-control policy. This attitude informs production-line work, rest periods, worker suspensions, and a variety of sophisticated human relations management techniques, including the organization of competitions, mini-Olympics, dances, meals, and outings.

The instability and insecurity of employment, the relative and absolute reduction of salaries (in terms of purchasing power), the slim to null possibility of improving one's position as a laborer, submission to the heavy demands and exacting rhythms of the labor process, the performance of routine manual tasks, and inadequate workplace safety and organization exemplify the prevailing labor conditions of thousands of women in the maquiladoras.

Note

1. Acids include nitric, sulfuric, hydrochloric, hydrofluoric, and chromic acids; common solvents include isopropyl alcohol, methyl alcohol, acetone, freon, hexane, trichloroethane, trichloroethylene, toluene, xylene, and methyl chloride.

3.

We Women Are More Responsible

Maquiladora work requires manual dexterity, a skill traditionally culti-
vated among women on the presumption that the very nature of the
feminine condition favors such ability. The rationale for employing
women in the maquiladoras is based on an ideological construct: the idea
of an essential female nature. The gendered supposition of a distinctive
biology and psychology naturalizes women's social condition; their
putative inferiority as intellectual and political actors purports to explain their vocation for and justifies their employment in the tedious and
repetitive labor required by the maquiladoras.

It is no accident that in the 128 maquiladoras that existed in Tijuana
in February 1982, women constituted 67.5 percent of all employees (SPP
1982). This phenomenon, which obtains throughout the industry, is
characteristic of the new international division of labor. Hiring women
has a concrete objective that Amelia and Alma imply in their testimony.
Yet the entrepreneurs manipulate the argument to veil the reality. As an
electronics maquiladora manager in Ciudad Juárez told me in March
1981, "Women have natural qualities that make them ideal for these
positions. Their delicate hands endow them with finesse and precision.
Moreover, the female psyche more easily endures the repetitive work."
Such affirmations reflect the firms' prevailing ideology. They try to
convince the workers and the population in general that women are
hired for their physical characteristics. They deny that this policy is
motivated by women's low degree of politicization and the advantages
this brings in terms of labor and production needs.

Plainly, women's physical characteristics cannot fully explain
maquiladora hiring practices. Hand size may be a biological reality—
although this trait is of no use for some manufacturers—but in the
maquiladoras this reality assumes ideological dimensions. The social
reality is that women generally have low levels of schooling and no work
experience, which denies them any conception of their rights as laborers.
The maquiladoras, in their very constitution, require more in terms of

hands-on human labor than mechanized production, more in the way of
a workforce than the technological means of production. The utilization
of female labor thus represents a guarantee in that it ensures production.
Said Ángela matter-of-factly:

> Work in the maquiladoras is oppressive, although it doesn't require
> brute strength. Indeed, it is easy work that you can quickly learn to
> do. It is light work *suited for women* [my emphasis]. We women
> are more serious in our attitude toward work. We're more respon-
> sible, which is why they only want female workers in the maquila-
> doras. At times, they have hired men for the work we do, but they
> haven't been up to the task because it's so tedious, and men are so
> awkward with their hands.

Turning back to the kitchen sink, Ángela continued:

> We can't deny that they hire women in the factories because we
> are more responsible in our work and more productive than men.
> Women work more quickly, men more slowly. Many employers
> say they hire women because we are more easily managed than
> men, but I don't think so. Maybe that was the case before, but now
> women don't tolerate as much in the workplace. The new ones,
> these young girls being hired every day, are more contentious than
> many of us old-timers. They don't let anything pass. They're more
> energetic.
>   I remember when I started working that it was almost three
> years before I allowed myself to relate to my co-workers. I just
> concentrated on my work. I worried when I didn't meet the pro-
> duction quota or when they called me on the carpet for something.
> I never went out with the rest of the crowd after work. But now,
> right away the girls make themselves at home. Their bosses come
> in and it doesn't faze them. And they don't bother to sit up straight
> or try to work rapidly. By contrast, when the boss came in, we used
> to sit as meek as lambs.
>   I think that as the younger ones have gotten some experience
> they're a lot less tolerant of supervision. Nowadays, if they start
> working somewhere and get called to task, they just walk off the
> job and find work somewhere else. Although people say it's diffi-
> cult to find work, I think for the young women from sixteen to
> twenty-two it's easy. There is so much turnover that there are
> always posters and announcements soliciting female workers.

Amelia, whose partner spent the majority of his time in the street,
spoke in a contemptuous tone:

We women are less problematic than men. We're more responsible. It's a real hardship if we lose our jobs. By contrast, men don't worry about it. If a man wakes up with a hangover some morning, just like that he blows off his job. We women tend not to have so many bad habits, and those women who do are less likely to blow it off— even if they're hung over, they go to work anyway. Some of my girlfriends say that they hire women because we're neat and dependable. Could be. The supervisors tell us they prefer women because we are patient and fastidious. Without patience and peace of mind it's impossible to do the work, as they tell us every day. It's so we don't get fed up, and so we'll continue doing the same old thing day after day.

The success of management discourse is widely evident. This fact is fundamental to understanding the generalized passivity of female maquiladora workers. The constant propaganda and scant alternatives effectively counteract the crushing monotony and exacting detail of conveyor-belt and assembly-line work.

Alma, momentarily silent, fixed her eyes on a photograph of herself as a young woman. Then she observed:

In the maquiladoras they hire women because men created more problems for them. We women are more easily managed. The bosses just have to express their concerns about production and we women, fools that we are, work even harder to protect their profits while we ourselves are dying of hunger. They break our spirit over any issue whatsoever. "Look, girls, the work is stacking up in Los Angeles from lack of sales. We're doing everything we can to move the dresses out so you won't be laid off, but you all have to help us out. How do you think we could raise your wages?" And, of course, we all forget about ourselves; we're powerless because we're divided, and in the absence of a labor union, they do with us as they wish. They always come up with a pretext to smooth things over and keep us under control.

By contrast, a male worker wouldn't stand for it—he's more aggressive. Men organize themselves, and if they don't get what they want, they walk off the job, which really inconveniences management. Under such conditions, the owners have to make concessions. That's why they pull in any young girl to work. They train them and pay them the minimum wage if they can. The owners well understand this; they don't hire men because the maquiladoras would not be as productive.

When I was working in the maquiladora, a number of us got together to discuss work, what they should be paying us, how they should be treating us. We had these meetings in a restaurant over coffee.

We women understand that we are more responsible and that this is partly why the factory owners prefer us as workers. Many maquiladora workers are single mothers and women whose husbands have abandoned them. It's not so easy for them to walk away from a job. This is an advantage for the owners because the girls have to provide for their children.

Many, the large majority of us, only went to primary school, which is why we have to take whatever work we can get. We can't afford the luxury of being too choosy about work. It wasn't because women didn't have the opportunity that many didn't go to school. Rather, it's because many Mexican women still embrace the idea that there is no reason to study if they are going to get married and be supported by their husband. So many times we've heard the girls say, "Now, I'm going to get married because I want to relax." And everything just gets worse for the poor girls because they end up with even more work, at home *and* in the factory.

I think a lot of men marry these women because they see they are workers, because with their job they can make an economic contribution to the household. Women just really get ground down. [Working a job and earning a salary do not exempt women from the domestic expectations men have of them.] The man has to prepare himself [educationally] to a much greater extent. Women also should prepare themselves because sometimes their luck is not so good and they have to go it alone.

Because most of us women are not qualified, we have to accept the worst work. I'm not here because I have chosen to be. I don't care for manual labor; it was the only opportunity I had.

Traditionally, Mexican women have not had consistent access to wage-labor experience. And when they do become wage earners, women's subject position in society is reproduced in prevailing relations of inequality between male employer and female employee. One way to avoid conflicts is to hire young women. The historical oppression of women—inscribed in relations of domination between husband and wife, father and daughter, brother and sister—has fostered a widespread attitude of docility and obedience among women. In capitalist societies, men have exercised power over women within and outside the nuclear family structure, in relationships that reinforce women's economic and sexual subordination.

Women's historical dependence has an ideological correlate: the supposition of a feminine essence whose naturalized qualities and roles are presumed to condition an aptitude or capacity for particular kinds of work. Hence, women in our society have grown up assimilating cultural standards of submission, self-denial, and resignation, together with qualities of modesty, patience, and reserve. All of these are seen as indispensable for maquiladora employment. These values attributed to women and transmitted through family life, schooling, and society in general condition the attitudes and norms of feminine behavior that the maquiladoras exploit to maximize production.

Obdulia was a married girl of seventeen, among the few female workers actually born in Tijuana. While she looked for something to give her seven-month-old son to make him stop crying, Obdulia commented in a low voice:

I never considered working in a factory. I always believed that my life would be centered in my home. Maybe that's why I was never interested in studying. What I wanted was to get married so I could stay at home all day tending to the household.

In my home, all the females had to help my mother around the house while the males had no household chores; all they had to do was study or go to work. Now, since I've gotten married, I have to work in the factory, care for my son, and maintain the house. As you can see, this room we live in isn't big; it always gets dirty and I'm constantly cleaning. For this room we pay 650 pesos [U.S.$20.00] a month in rent. We share the only bathroom with twelve other rooms, and we get along well with our neighbors. We have to wash the dishes outside in the laundry sinks, because there is no water in the room. We hang our clothes to dry in the adjoining vacant lot.

I have to get up at 5:00 in the morning to take my son to my sister's house. I take him so early that my sister is still asleep. I put my son in bed, and there he stays until 7:30 A.M., when my sister gets up to begin her daily chores.

When I get out of work at 5:00 in the afternoon I go straight to pick up my boy, then I go to buy something to give him to eat. As you see, I have to put aside a part of my salary to buy milk for my son and some vegetables for stewing, to eat with beans and tortillas. My money almost never goes far enough to be able to afford any meat. I go home to cook, tidy the house, and give my husband, Martín, something to eat. The poor guy comes home dying of hunger. After that I wash the dishes while Martín steps outside to chat with our neighbors on the block. And around 10:00 we go to bed.

Saturdays I wash all the clothes and put the house in order. Martín works Saturday mornings, comes home around midday, and then goes out with his buddies to see a movie or go dancing. I go

with my son to see one of my sisters. On Sunday I visit my mother
and Martín goes out again with his friends. We don't usually go out
together because there's no place to leave the boy. But yesterday
my mother took care of him and Martín and I went out dancing
together. Frequently, all the girls from the factory go out dancing
together to the Río Rita Club. I never go with them because Martín
never gives me the chance. Going out dancing allows you to think
less about work and housekeeping.

Housekeeping, like factory work, is a repetitive and interminable task
that by no means favors the development of one's intellectual or creative
capacity. Work in the factory and at home represents a double shift for
women; it is obligatory work, although household tasks are not compensated monetarily and rarely accorded social value.

Clearly, employment in the maquiladora or any other industry does
not make housework more attractive and does not liberate women from
the responsibility of domestic work (Costa and James 1979: 14). It is also
plain that the idea of spending one's life doing electrical wiring, assembly, soldering, or sewing is untenable. The majority of female workers
reject these things in various ways and resist doing them. There can be
no doubt that the ensuing struggles, at the individual or collective level,
spring from receiving a paycheck. While they detest their jobs and the
conditions under which they labor, work in the maquiladora is their first
experience with social independence, an opportunity for female migrants to expand the limited worldview of their place of origin, and for
women in general to leave behind their domestic isolation. Alma
observed:

When I think about work I realize that the disadvantages outweigh
the advantages. They pay us badly and endanger our health, and
the work is boring and tedious. We have no job security, we are
stuck in the factory so much of the time that we have no time to
do anything else, and we can't take care of our children and homes
as we should. We have to get up very early in the morning, then I
spend the entire day in a bad mood, angry and annoyed. And when
they make decisions, they don't take my needs into account. Still,
I've gotten to know a lot of people, and I've learned to make
demands, and to recognize the problems of women and of all of us
who work. I've learned that we should struggle in unity.

In this respect, employment in any industry has its positive aspects.
In the factory, women come to see what they considered to be their life's
destiny in a social context and see that they share problems. They

communicate with one another and transcend the level of mere family complaints. Their experience in the maquiladora enables them to understand that their own particular life circumstances are not the product of bad luck, poverty, the number of children they have, or an alcoholic husband; rather, these phenomena are the product of the broader social system (de Leonardo 1976: 22). For many of the maquiladora workers who are migrants or single mothers or both, their employment signifies economic "independence." They achieve this independence via a total dependence on the paycheck, however, because in many cases the woman's salary is the household's only source of income. The majority of migrant female workers assert and believe that to make it to Tijuana and work in the maquiladoras has been an improvement, as they have freed themselves of the influence of their father, mother, brother, or husband.

As a woman begins working outside the home, she gains a sense of independence as she gains some authority and control with regard to household decisions. By maintaining or helping maintain the household in economic and material terms, she has a greater say in what to do with her money and participates to a greater degree in other family matters that had been the province of the husband or other male household head. So as a woman begins to participate in economically productive activity, behavioral patterns change, modifying the family structure in some ways, without, however, diminishing women's own exploitation or oppression.

4.

Maquila *Muchachas:*
Pretty Young Maids

By conscripting young females from a specified socioeconomic sector, maquiladoras have created a unique workforce. As Jorge Carrillo and Alberto Hernández (1981, 1982a, 1982b) note, cultivating this sector is not simply a matter of employing the most productive workers; it targets a category of workers whose age and gender ensure a consistent lack of workplace experience. This strategy facilitates their replacement without creating serious labor problems. The characteristics of the maquiladora workforce are not accidental; they result from a careful hiring policy in which the firms seek to maintain effective control of labor and a high level of worker exploitation. It is also notable that 68 percent of the fifty women we interviewed in Tijuana in 1982 were between the ages of sixteen and twenty-five. This is in line with Gambrill's (1981) finding of 61 percent in her 1977 study.

To observe shift change at the maquiladora is to be reminded of the end of the day as students pour out of their secondary or girls' preparatory schools, smiling in response to the bell that signals their temporary liberation. Some girls hang around while others run to catch a truck or van waiting to begin its route. What stands out are the tweed pants and the brilliantly colored blouses; many of the women appear not to have put in a full eight or ten hours' work. They have carefully made up their faces before leaving the factories, especially if it is Friday and a group of girlfriends is heading out to dance or have a drink.

During a meeting to discuss some of the problems of the maquiladoras, Elena offered, with some irritation, the following commentary:

> The maquiladora owners aren't stupid. The damned bosses only want sweet young things, girls under nineteen. They say that in many firms, when the girls turn twenty, the bosses start to look for ways to dismiss them.
>
> The only good thing about the supervisor we have at the moment is that he's not obsessed with age. All he demands is that we be good workers. He handles everyone on equal terms.

The other women laughed in derision at the double entendre. Elena inhaled to still her laughter and continued:

There was one time when the factory said they didn't want fat girls because they couldn't stand up to the heat and produce at the same level. Who knows if it's true? What they wanted was pretty young things who dressed nicely. If you were poorly dressed when you went to look for a job they turned you down.

Margarita, a plump thirty-year-old matron, commented:

It's a good thing they changed that policy. If not, none of us would have been able to land a job here.

They all laughed again. In a tone of spirited annoyance, Elena added:

I remember when I was trying for a job, the head of personnel turned to another administrator and asked, "How do you like these girls?" And they looked us up and down. If they thought you were pretty, you got a job; if not, no way. It wasn't like we were going out dancing; we were going to be working and getting screwed!

María Cristina confided in the youthful tone of one scarcely past her eighteenth birthday:

The maquiladoras have given work to a lot of us girls who needed it, and if it weren't for this type of business, I don't know what we would do for work. I think that since the maquiladoras were established here in Tijuana there are fewer idlers.

Commented Obdulia:

I started working when I was sixteen. I remember that right after my son was born I asked my husband for permission to go with a girlfriend to find a job. We arrived at a factory, they asked us some questions, and they gave me a job, but not her. I was really nervous. It was something new for me because I had never worked before.

Hiring young women has not decreased, as many entrepreneurs have claimed, the amount of surplus labor. To the contrary, this reserve labor force grows day by day, as it has for some time, because of demographic growth, the influx of migrant women attracted by the maquiladora industry, women's short working lives, and changes in the production regime. This abundant labor force without work has facilitated the selection of a specific category of working women who achieve the maximum yield.

To try to understand personnel selection, I applied for a job in a maquiladora in Ciudad Juárez. I went to the firm that was interviewing and asked for an application. The form asked for, among other things, my name and that of my parents, their occupations, my work history, education level, date and place of birth, and the reasons I sought a job.

The office was small, full of the diplomas of the head of personnel. There were also diplomas and trophies awarded to the firm, and photos in which a number of girls appeared with the maquiladora owners and managers standing around a trophy. The girls were in their bright sports uniforms, and the men were very jaunty with their big smiles.

In the outer office there was a secretary who treated me and all the other applicants like little girls. She addressed us as "little girl" or "princess," or with a patronizing, "What can I do for you, dearie?" After I had filled out the application and handed it back, they sent me to interview with the plant psychologist. She called me by my first name, and I continued to detect an attitude reserved for someone considered less than capable.

She asked me where I was from, what had brought me to the city, who had referred me for the job, with whom I was living, my level of schooling, and other general information. She commented that I seemed different from the other workers and that perhaps that would cause me some problems in the beginning: "They're not bad; later on they'll treat you better. Many things are said of the girls who work in these factories, but it's not true. The poor behavior of a few workers has created a bad reputation for which everyone has had to pay."

The psychologist was plainly referring to the large number of single mothers and to comments that the firms have encouraged to denigrate the figure of the working woman and to augment competitiveness between us. Yet the psychologist expounded a distinct argument:

The North American culture that comes to us via TV and film has strongly affected the morality of the girls; this is quite different from the situation in other regions away from the northern frontier of our country. These girls, because they lack education, adopt some of the foreign customs they see in films, but without taking the necessary precautions, and without really understanding what they're doing. Under that influence, these girls go out one night with a guy and they go to bed with him. An enormous number of girls have had frequent sexual relations, but they don't want to take birth control. Did you know that this city has had a rise in the divorce index? Every day there are more single mothers, and the large majority have to work in the maquiladoras in order to raise their children. Apart from that, the city is growing rapidly due to migration.

The unspoken intention of her words and tone of voice was to convince me that I shouldn't have children. For the firm, each worker's child implies a lowering of productivity and extra expenditures in the form of disability payments during the final months of pregnancy. At that moment, I remembered the following lines from Octavio Paz: "The methods of mass production apply as well to ethics, art, and emotions" (1982:182).

After the interview I remained in the lobby, waiting for the required aptitude test. It covered addition, subtraction, multiplication, common fractions, number series, synonyms, and word-play problems. Then I had a second interview with a supervisor. About twenty-five years old, he had completed half of his engineering studies at the Instituto Politécnico Nacional and finished at the Tecnológico in Ciudad Juárez: "What is the highest grade you finished in school?"

"Third year in secondary school," I replied, trying to say as little as possible.

Pacing around his office with the air of a potentate, he asked, "Do you have any soldering experience?"

"No, but I think I could learn."

"Let's see," he said.

He walked over to a shelf and picked up a board about thirty centimeters [12 inches] long and set with a row of rods. He handed me some pieces of plastic sheathing that almost covered the rods. He told me to put the sheathing on the rods as quickly as possible, then remove and replace them again. As I did so he timed me with a stopwatch. I was a little bit nervous—he never stopped talking, but I had to concentrate and work quickly if I wanted the job.

After I finished the test, he began to tell me about the work in his section, the production of cable TV transistors. Without telling me how I had done, he dismissed me. A half hour later I had my medical exam. While waiting, I spoke with a woman about thirty years old who had bronchitis; she had been given leave from work, but without pay. The firm's argument was that her bronchitis was not a work-related illness. She told me that, even though she wasn't completely well, she wanted to return to work, not so much for the money but because she didn't like being cooped up at home, where her kids were "always fighting."

The doctor asked what diseases my parents and I had had. Then he asked me if I were a "*señorita*"—that is, a virgin—if I had frequent sexual relations, the date of my last menstrual period, if I were regular, if I suffered from upset stomach, and so forth. He examined my mouth, took my blood pressure, listened to my heart, and palpated my abdomen to make sure I was not pregnant.

Several minutes after the exam the secretary told me they had accepted me. I was to come back the next day with my birth certificate and primary school diploma in order to sign my contract, after which they would explain the factory rules to me.

The next day I showed up with five other young women, all between the ages of sixteen and twenty-three, and a young man of around twenty-five. They showed us into the locker room, and the same supervisor who had interviewed us quickly read us the factory regulations, so quickly that we didn't catch any of it. It was apparent that his instructions were intentionally brisk; they didn't want us to completely grasp how we were supposed to conduct ourselves. Nobody dared to speak up when he asked, "Any questions?" I didn't say anything either, as I wanted things to take their own course. We were told to show up the following Monday at 5:40 A.M., in order to begin working at 6:00 A.M.

Apparently, not all the women who want to get a job in a maquiladora are subject to the same procedure. It depends on how technologically sophisticated the plant is and how critical it is in economic terms. The simpler the operations involved, the less complicated and demanding are the application process and the work regime. In their job interviews these firms seek those characteristics that best fill their needs. For the owners it is very important that the applicants not be pregnant, which explains the medical exam and all the questions related to one's sex life. The psychologist has her own way of proceeding, presenting herself as a friend in whom you can confide. She creates an ambience of confidence and trust. The physician interrogates you in the manner of a judge. The supervisor picks you apart with his gaze.

The business is interested in two fundamental issues: productivity and quality. A pregnant woman is not going to produce at the same level as a woman who is not pregnant. Pregnancy entails an extra expenditure because the firm is required to compensate the woman for a three-month maternity leave. For the firm—which subscribes to the motto "Time is money"—maternity leave constitutes a lapse during which the laborer is unproductive.

Still, even with all the conditions that must be met to be hired, and despite a labor policy geared to employing single women, who are seen as less likely to become pregnant, the composition of the workforce is in constant flux because most marriages and pregnancies occur between ages sixteen and twenty-five—the age range within which most workers fall.

María Cristina commented:

Most of the girls who work in the factory have children. On Mothers' Day the bosses gave a flower to all the women with children, so the majority had a flower. There are very few of us who are not mothers, and that's because we're very young. A lot of us were surprised because we thought there were many women without kids. Of the 350 women working in the factory, I'd say that 300 are mothers. I think that now it's easier to have a child because you earn your own money, and that helps you feel more independent. A lot of women have children because they want to have them, and not because they screwed up, some maybe because they weren't careful. A lot of women have children because Social Security gives them a stipend. They give you one payment before birth and another afterward. It seems like they give a good bit of money; I think it's over twenty thousand pesos [U.S.$762.00 in January; $134.00 at year-end].

Social Security charges the factory, which is why the factory doesn't like it when we get pregnant. Why do you think that, when we apply for a job, the first thing they do is the medical exam? It's to be sure you're not pregnant. Some of us are being sent to the doctor so he can check us again. He's a private doctor who sees all of us who work in the factory. He asks us a lot of questions and takes a medical history: heart exam, blood pressure, and vision, and he asks if we have diabetes. We get paid for the time we have to go to the doctor; every day they send three women to the doctor by appointment. The boss calls the clinic to let them know who is being sent over, and when we're done the doctor calls the factory to say we're done and that we're returning to work. They really keep an eye on us because they say they are paying us for that time. One day a woman took more time than necessary to return to the factory, and they really got on her case. After such an incident you can be dismissed for any little thing.

The managers get really angry if they learn that someone is pregnant. Still, it happens a lot in the factory. Everywhere I look I see big bellies.

Some of the girls leave their kids with whoever will take care of them. Those whose mothers also live here in Tijuana don't have as many problems because they leave their kids with them. Otherwise, a woman has to pay someone a lot of money to take care of her kids. A lot of women spend a third of their salary on child care. Others without anyone to care for their children, or without enough money to pay someone, leave their kids locked up alone at home so they can't go out, and they turn off the electricity so the kids won't electrocute themselves. Some give their kids tranquilizers to sedate them and keep them from getting into trouble.

Many of these women are single mothers, women who struggle daily for their children's and their own survival. They continue to be bound by the prejudices and moral expectations of their employers, other workers, neighbors, and even their relatives, who characterize them as "easy" or as "women of ill repute." Some supervisors and bosses have taken advantage of this situation to pressure the women.

This contempt for women conforms with ideological distortions based on, among other things, the reproductive function, which rationalizes the marginalization of women. An atmosphere of shame, scorn, anxiety, and emotional blackmail has kept women from asking why they should bear the responsibility for child care while they work. They don't believe that the employer or the state has an obligation to provide child care services. In none of the Tijuana maquiladoras has there been a movement to create a child care center run by the workers themselves, although in the city of Tijuana alone there were over six thousand female workers with children in 1982.

In terms of educational level, virtually all of the women have finished primary school, as the primary certificate is required for employment in every maquiladora. It thus is possible to capitalize on a degree of academic preparation at no cost to the enterprise, even though the work requires a minimum capability.

It is important to note that the primary school is precisely where the traditional image is reproduced of the teacher as the authority, the one who gives orders, the one who governs truth and reason. The student learns to be patient and obedient and not to question anything he or she is told to do; in short, the student is taught to obey. This conditioning— which reflects the prevailing conditions of life at home and in school— is exploited and reinforced in the factory, as seen in the relations between the bosses and female workers.

Around 28 percent of the women interviewed had taken vocational courses for six months or longer in areas including sewing, tailoring, cosmetology, business, typing, and English. The majority had developed skills in those areas. In a sense, the firms have also benefited from this training, although the majority of women involved believe their training has been of no personal benefit. Indeed, they did not even list their vocational certificates on their job applications because they did not consider them important.

The women with vocational qualifications, like the majority of female employees, tend to be adaptable workers. Because they consider

After long and exhausting hours of work, the women received minimal nourishment from the mobile food trucks, due to the lack of cafeterias in the maquiladoras.

A workers' meeting during the strike.

themselves to be unqualified, they are more versatile than male workers. They are as capable of gluing and willing to glue circuit boards and solder resistors as they are of sweeping the factory, serving coffee, or sewing on a button for a supervisor or a boss; they are simply doing what they learned to do so well at home, in school, or in vocational training.

The household is the essential site of consumption, social conditioning, and social production; it also serves as a labor reserve. It is a center of production in that it produces and reproduces the human being, that is, the worker. The household also functions to create men and women who adapt to the system and disciplines them to fulfill gender roles that are socially defined in accordance with a system of values or ideology that reflects the interests of the dominant class.

The dominant ideology dictates that within the household structure the woman's life should revolve around her children and husband, which isolates her from the rest of the world. This is why one so commonly hears the workers remark, "They always told me at home and in school that my life would involve being at home, taking care of my children, attending to my husband, and maintaining the home." It is easy to understand how the household, as a mechanism of socialization, fixes, maintains, and reproduces the image of the deferential, obedient, domesticated woman.

By fostering the acquisition and transmission of knowledge, skills, attitudes, and values consistent with the system, schools also encourage women to reaffirm, internalize, and preserve the attitudes that condition women's roles and their participation in society. Formal education must be understood as a conscious process of instruction and apprenticeship that is controlled, correctable, and replicable. This process perpetuates the traditional image of women and, more generally, the image of women as the vehicle for transmitting all those everyday values characteristic of a society vigorously dedicated to consumption and fostering those values most fundamental to capitalism: competition, individualism, selfishness, love of money, and upward mobility, among others. These values are reinforced inside the maquiladoras via control mechanisms directed toward women and predicated on those feminine roles imposed by society at large.

Work experience is one factor the firms have taken advantage of, and it is always considered when selecting personnel. For 52 percent of those interviewed, the maquiladora represented their first factory experience. The remaining 48 percent had prior experience primarily in domestic service, or in small commercial establishments. Only 12 percent of the women interviewed had previously worked in another industrial sector (primarily packinghouses and factories producing candy or cookies).

This lack of experience is one of the reasons female workers accept adverse working conditions. They have no frame of reference because they have not had the opportunity to gain experience that might enable them to better organize themselves and confront their situation. Few workers resist working under such conditions, and fewer still arise in organized opposition. One can hear plenty of conversation in the dining halls or in the street at quitting time, but in the majority of cases, it takes the form of complaining among the workers themselves. These informal discussions and conversations constitute a hint, a sign of life, a latent spirit of struggle that may eventually express itself in informal or formal organizations.

The collective predicament is diluted in an infinite series of individual situations, which impedes the discovery of concrete elements of mutual support on which to build a broader struggle. Two opposing sentiments reside in the consciousness of almost all the female workers: they cultivate a certain sense of gratitude toward the boss and the factory for having hired them and given them the opportunity to earn a salary, secure medical attention, and raise their standing on the social scale; they also feel a certain disdain as they endure the disgrace of being stuck for so many hours in the factory repeating the same boring, painful, and fatiguing movement a thousand and one times.

All of the women have devised personal solutions: get married, return to their home village, move on to another factory. Few think about uniting in struggle because they consider their working lives as a secondary activity, a temporary alternative, or, in the best of cases, preparation for their core role as mothers and wives.

Notes

1. Although Margarita was not one of my ten case studies, I have included her here because she participated in this discussion.

2. This finding is by no means representative of the reality, as it is based on only fifty random interviews, but in any case, it is highly suggestive of prevailing trends.

3. Domestic service is defined here following Gambrill (1981) and is characterized by the provision of personal services under conditions of unstable, nonclassified, low-paying employment.

5.

Who I Am, Where I Come From, and Where I'm Going

Origins

Sixty-eight percent of the workers interviewed were migrants. They came principally from other parts of Baja California and from Jalisco, Durango, Sinaloa, Michoacán, Sonora, Nayarit, and Guanajuato. Of these, 73 percent came in search of better living conditions. Some came after the father went to the United States and saved enough money to bring the entire family. Others came with their abandoned or widowed mothers to "get ahead in life." They had heard it was easier to secure work in Tijuana. Twenty-seven percent of the migrants came unaccompanied in search of work, attracted by the maquiladoras, "those industries that were offering work to women like us." Various interviewees framed it this way: "I came on vacation and I liked it; here I could find work."

María Luisa

I was born in the mountains of Durango, where I lived until I was eleven. My father worked the land, my mother dedicated herself to the household, and we helped her with the animals, the cows, goats, sheep, pigs, and chickens. Some of these we sold and the rest we kept. I don't know how much land my father had, but he grew corn, beans, and potatoes. What we produced was for us, but if the yield allowed, we sold some of the harvest.

My village was quite isolated and without services. The mail still does not reach our village; there is no electricity or anything else. People call it the village of Matatitos, but they also call it Rancho Nuevo. It's in the State of Durango.

We were very poor. Sometimes the corn harvest was abundant, but at times the harvest failed. There was only our house and two others, but quite separated from each other. The municipal center was not too far away, within an hour's walk. They had bullfighting there, horse races, and displays of horsemanship. There were more people there, but in our hamlet there is practically nobody. It's still quite isolated there.

We were a family of eight: five daughters, my parents, and my grandfather. We assisted my father as if we were men, and we spent most of our time helping out. My two older sisters completed fourth grade in primary school, but I almost didn't go to school at all. I didn't like it. The school was quite far off, in another village, and we had to walk there every day, early in the morning, then walk home again in the afternoon. To get there took us forty-five minutes, to get back home, an hour. Going there was downhill, so it was easy, but returning was all uphill, and I got very tired. Sometimes I went to school, and sometimes I didn't.

At home my eldest sister ground the corn, my sister and I hauled the water, and we helped my grandfather in the corral. My father was hardly ever around. He was the breadwinner and he was always on the go. He always left the house and didn't come back. I'd say he had a wild streak. Our grandfather lived with us, and he was the one who actually took charge of things, because my father died when I was around six years old, so then we were left with my grandfather. My eldest sister is two years older than the next sister, and I was five years older than my next sister, because there was a brother in between us who died.

Then my grandfather died, which affected me deeply because my mother started to think about getting married again. As long as my grandfather was alive she never thought about it, or at least she never said so, but soon after my grandfather passed away, she did remarry. She was thirty-five years old at the time. When she told us she was getting married again, I didn't want to live there any longer.

Then an opportunity to leave presented itself. One of my sisters had come to Tijuana and stayed for a year with some of my mother's close friends, and they brought my sister back to the village around the time my mother announced her marriage intentions. My mother's friends asked if we knew anyone who might want to come to Tijuana, and I told them I wanted to go. My mother told me that if I wanted to, then I should go to Tijuana. She never told me no; she didn't keep us from going wherever we wanted to go. I was twelve years old and I was going to live with this old couple and do as they told me to do. They assumed responsibility for me, to provide what they could for me.

I was quite happy. I wanted to come and get to know the place, even when my sister told me, "Don't go, because it's going to be

tough for you." She told me she had had a very bad time and
pressed me not to go, but I said to her, "No matter how bad, hell or
high water, I'm going." So the old couple lectured me about how
they wouldn't tolerate any crying or complaining on my part, and I
said I wasn't going to return from Tijuana soon, so they took me. I
came with the old couple to Mazatlán by bus, and from there by
train to Tijuana.

I didn't know anything about Tijuana. I had never been in a city.
I had never left the village, and the village wasn't very big! So it
was quite an experience to go to Mazatlán and take the train.
Everything seemed beautiful to me.

I got to Tijuana and I couldn't pronounce a lot of words. I
couldn't pronounce "carpet," or "linoleum," or "newspaper." I
didn't even know these things existed. The old lady's niece told
me, "You don't say it like that! You say it this way." She taught
me how to pronounce the words correctly. I was really taken with
TV because I had never seen it. I had seen movies, because there
was a man who brought them to show in the village. I had only
seen movies, that was it. But I had never imagined there could be
this little box, you turn it on, and there are people talking. I really
liked TV. It's very entertaining!

The old couple enrolled me in school. They had some little
houses that they rented, and they lived off the rent, plus whatever
their two nephews sent them. I worked for them until I was
fourteen, doing all the household chores. Everything! I washed,
ironed, and cleaned. The lady could hardly do anything by that
time, so I did it all. I was also taken with the washing machine;
when it came time for the laundry, it saved me a lot of work. I was
also the one who went out to do the shopping. They showed me
how to get to the store.

There is a friend I still visit, a nurse I got to know in the hospital
where I was operated on. She told me her brother could arrange for
me to get a passport. I told her I didn't have a birth certificate, just
a voucher of birth registration. My birth certificate was in a village
called Tayoltita, some distance from my hamlet, because that's
where the records were sent. She told me her brother had a lot of
pull and that he could arrange everything with just the registration
voucher.

And so it was. I went with her and her brother took me to the
queue, where the Mexican officials gave me Form 13.[1] Then I dealt
with the U.S. officials, and they gave me the border-crossing card,
which I wanted so I could work on the other side.

I was fourteen then, and the old man with whom I was living had died, leaving the old lady alone. I left to work on the other side with one of the nurse's acquaintances. In the house where I worked I did all the chores for a married couple and their three children. I cleaned and the lady of the house did the cooking. I worked for them for six months, and then I returned to Rancho Nuevo to see my mother. I was fifteen years old by then.

I was home for two weeks, then I returned with my eldest sister, the one who had already been here to Tijuana. Her husband had abandoned her, so she also brought her two-month-old daughter with her.

We went to the old lady's house, where I left my sister and her daughter. She helped the old lady, cleaning the house and keeping her company. I went to the other side, where I found a better-paying job and sent them money. A year and a half later, the old lady's daughter arrived. She was going to go with my sister to Rancho Nuevo again, and I also decided to accompany them.

I stayed there for two weeks. My mother was still living with my stepfather. He and I didn't care for one another. When I got back home, he left the house. I didn't like him because I had a sister who had been ill from birth. When she walked she fell down all the time because she didn't have her five senses; she wasn't aggressive, but he always mistreated her. He'd send her to do something and because she didn't do it quickly he abused her a lot. I called him on it, and my mother got angry at me. That's why I didn't spend much time there. They had five more children, so the house was always full of people.

Later I returned to the other side and got another job through friends I had there. They gave me the telephone number of someone who needed help; I called and spoke with them and they gave me a job. Also, the lady for whom I had first worked on the other side told me, "Now that you've come back, I'm going to find you a job that pays better," and she recommended me to some other ladies. I continued working there, and when I turned eighteen I came back.

But one time when I went back home, my bag was stolen with everything in it, including my border-crossing card. So I came to Tijuana and reported the loss, and they made me wait six months for a new one. At that point I didn't want to be in Tijuana because I could do better being on the other side. A lady got me across without a border-crossing card by saying I was her daughter. I stayed there for about six months. There was a lot of housework, and I had to do everything, even the laundry sometimes. The work was demanding, but the people treated me well; they paid me in dollars and I worked at my own pace.

I came back to Mexico and no longer felt like returning to the other side. Without my border-crossing card, it was more difficult to cross the border, even though they were less strict then than they are now. Before, with a border-crossing card you could go as far as Los Angeles and nobody hassled you like they do now. You have to have papers to get any farther than San Diego, and everywhere you go they're after you. I stayed in Tijuana and met my future husband. We met in the Independencia district of Tijuana, and every time I was back in town we would see one another, until we became sweethearts.

Here in Tijuana I was working in the home of the old lady's daughter-in-law. Then I went to live with a girl who some time before had come from Rancho Nuevo also to work as a domestic. She suggested that I move in with her, so I did. Because I needed money, I went to work in a maquiladora.

I told my boyfriend that I wanted to work in a factory, and he told me to go see his uncle, who was a maquiladora administrator. I met with him, he gave me a recommendation and told me to take it to the office, where they would give me a job. And they did.

In the maquiladora they didn't give me any exams; I just filled out the application. I knew nothing of factory work; I wasn't interested in the question like I am now. When I worked on the other side I didn't know that the maquiladoras even existed. The girls who had worked for the old lady were working in the factory by then. When I told them I was going to work on the other side, they said, "The factory is hiring. Why not stay and get a job here?" I applied, but I had no idea what the work involved.

From the beginning I got along well with the other factory workers because what I wanted to do was work. It was different from domestic employment, where you work alone at your own rhythm. In the factory there were a lot of people and everything had to be done rapidly. In those days I made nineteen dollars a week, because they used to pay in dollars.

When I started working in the factory I knew it would be for a while, because they told me that with proof of employment it was easier to get a border-crossing card. And so it was—I got the card on that basis.

After that I didn't go to the other side because I got married, and we went to live in a little house near the factory where I worked. My husband was the manager of a supermarket, and with what he earned we managed to make a living. I kept on working; it was important to me because that way I could continue to help my mother. I always sent her money, and I still do.

After I was married I brought one of my sisters, who helped me with the house while I went to the factory. I stayed at the job for something over a year, but because I got pregnant shortly after starting there, I got subsidized maternity leave, and only shortly after I returned to work they closed the factory because the rest of the girls went on strike. They say the factory closed because of the strike. The owners left—that was in 1970. I didn't take part in the strike. I wasn't so inclined because the administrators had other factories, and they told us, "If you stay out of the strike we can find you work elsewhere." I was more interested in working than I was in the strike, and within two months of the factory closing, they found something for us elsewhere. Those administrators could hire us because they control five or six factories, even though each one has a different owner.

When it closed, the factory had about four hundred workers, and only one hundred were on strike. Those of us who weren't on strike went every day to the administrators' new offices and they gave us bus fare. While the others were fighting, we reported at the office. The administrators told us a new factory was about to open and that they were going to take care of us.

It didn't affect me much to be without work because my husband gave me money for the household expenses. I was without work for about two months, and when the new factory opened they called me to work. They did some very exacting soldering work, so they only had people with soldering experience. The factory people taught us how to solder. They gave us a course in soldering, and they gave us diplomas.

After I was there for three years they closed the factory because they said it was what they had to do. Nobody complained. Some approached the administrators, who gave them work in other factories. I got a job in another electronics plant, but this was rare; most were not rehired.

In the factory the supervisors were women, and we got along well. At times they were bossy, but I always got along with them. Those who didn't get into the routine would be called down, but because I didn't like being reprimanded I always tried to do my job well. After I worked there for two years the factory moved out around Mexicali, and they found me a job in another factory in Tijuana, where for seven years I did the same kind of work.

Since coming to Tijuana I've learned a lot of new things and met

a lot of people. I make my money and I can help out my husband.
Whenever I think about my past I realize that I've changed a lot
since I came to Tijuana.

As we have seen, work is a necessity for every one of the women
employed in the maquiladoras. Working conditions do not guarantee
even minimal conditions of health, workplace and occupational safety,
and job security. Job insecurity profoundly conditions workers' social
behavior. Hence, their individual interests outweigh any perception of
the collective interests necessary to forge a unified perception of working-class consciousness. That María Luisa preferred not to participate in
the strike clearly demonstrates how the difficult social and employment
situation of women in the maquiladora constrains their participation in
the strike movement. We might say that María Luisa was the typical
"scab." Yet I believe that her attitude must be viewed from the perspective of the contradictions manifest in the heterogeneity of working-class
experience, of the disarticulation of labor, ideological manipulation by
the corporation and the class in power, and so forth.

Ángela

It might seem like I exaggerate, but it gave me a great sense of
happiness to start working at the maquiladora; I thought I had
overcome my past. It was the moment in which God heard my
prayers and changed my life. I could forget what was behind me.
That part of my life was so very difficult that on one occasion I
threw myself in front of a car, and on another I took a bunch of
pills. What I wanted was to die.

I was born in Comala in 1939. Comala was a small town and I
didn't live there very long, because at a young age I went to live
with my sister in Colima. She lived there because she had married
a Colima man who was a tanner. From the age of seven I lived with
them, went to school there through the sixth grade, and stayed
with them until I was fourteen.

When I got home from school I helped my sister by doing
errands like carrying water, because in those days there was no
piped water. I had to carry a bucket from the water taps located
on the street corner. My sister has a daughter six months younger
than me, so we were almost twins. She, her brother, and I went
every weekend to my parents' home, the farm. We went in a big
stakebed truck that was covered in the back. We left Friday after-
noons at 3:00, right after school. It took us three hours of driving
because it was a narrow road.

We were eight children in all, and I was the youngest. My father was a farmer, but the land was not his. I played among the trees and helped my father plant beans and corn. We also planted vegetables, radishes, chiles, and all that. I took care of the pigs and chickens we had, because my mother loved having animals. I often amused myself by riding horses or harvesting cucumbers or green corn.

I liked going to the farm on weekends, but I didn't like living there. I was the only one in the family who didn't like the country, but it was a nice place to rest and to play.

When I left the farm to live with my sister, my father was an administrator for a very rich Colima family named Cárdenas, who had a mill on the outskirts of town, although now it's surrounded by the city. The mill where my father worked was like a modern hacienda, where they ground corn and rice. It was also a granary, because they stored a lot of corn and rice. My brother-in-law offered this job to my father and he accepted because he was very hard-working. My father was in the Revolution, and then he was a member of the *cristero* movement,[2] but when peace was negotiated he had to leave the village near Guadalajara where he was born. By the end of the war my parents already had three children. People told my father that the government was going to finish off all the surviving *cristeros*, and my mother was so terrified that she said, "Let's go away to Comala, darling!"

We would fall asleep listening to our father tell his tales. We loved to hear him talk; it was like a story. My father told us that "the general"[3] distributed many things among his people; the assistant called roll and to each one he gave his due. They gave my father a good bit of money, about fifty horses and mules, and close to two hundred head of cattle. All this was taken from the families they had sacked. My father was "the general's" bodyguard.

He told us that he felt bad about receiving things that he hadn't won by the sweat of his brow. It was very difficult for him because he had always been a devout Catholic. My father gave away the cattle and horses and most of the money. He kept only a small amount, which at the time was still worth a lot.

In Comala they bought a big adobe house. It had a lot of rooms, a kitchen, and a big corridor. He opened a grocery store there, and they built it up. They prospered even though they gave credit. People paid by the week or the month. They owed him a lot of money, and he kept a notebook with figures and names of those in his debt. He kept good accounts because he was very astute. Nothing left the store without being accounted for. My father remained in Comala until the Cárdenas family offered him the position in Colima.

He sold everything, the house and the store, and he left to become administrator of the mill, which had many employees. My brothers also worked there, milking the cows. One of my brothers died there when he was nineteen.

There in Colima my father had everything. They even gave him a house, but he worked a lot and made many millions for the Cárdenas family. He used his brain, he got very tired, and they paid him very little. My mother and sisters worked in the house, and they saw my father very little.

Mr. Salvador Cárdenas died, and his sons wanted my father to keep working in the mill, but by then my father no longer wanted to work day and night. He spoke with my brothers and told them to quit as well. So they left for a hamlet in Comala. They weren't paid anything there, but my father might as well have been the owner. He had cows and horses and worked the land. They could sell whatever they produced. Although they had everything, I preferred to live with my sister.

When I went to primary school I wanted to be a teacher, and I think that I could have been one because I always liked to study. Unfortunately, my mother died and I couldn't continue studying.

Before my mother died my father had already stopped working, but my mother continued. She sold clothing, and I went with her whenever I could. She bought bolts of fabric, shawls, and special orders in Colima and sold them in the hamlet. She was paid in eggs, one or two hundred eggs by each customer. At the end of the day, with six or eight hundred eggs, we went by bus to Colima to sell them. She was a trader and I was the escort who watched out for her.

I was eleven years old when my mother died. My father was quite elderly by then, and he lived with my brothers. They had land, but everything went to take care of my mother. Because my father was elderly, and a country man, my brothers didn't want him to work with my brother-in-law in Colima because he was too old to be a mason. We were in pretty bad shape and deep in debt, but my father told us, "I'm going back to the country; I can't stand to be here. You all decide if you're coming with me or if you're staying." I decided to stay because I didn't like the country, and even less so without my mother. My sister who was single also stayed, and my brothers trained as masons to work with my brother-in-law in Colima.

My father went to the country by himself, but he stayed there for only three months before returning to Colima, where my brothers took care of him. I cleaned house and washed the clothes. I carried the big laundry basket to the river, a half hour's walk, where I remained from 6:30 in the morning until 7:00 in the evening washing. My sister went off to work, and she also had to take care of my brothers and my father. She made tortillas, cooked their meals, and cleaned the entire house.

By the age of fourteen I already had a boyfriend. He was twenty-six years old, and he had a lot of patience with me, but I soon broke off with him and then became the sweetheart of the father of my children. He was a truck driver, and I finally married him when I was twenty.

When I was fifteen I had gone to live with a woman who spoke with my father and asked him to send me with her to help her and keep her company. My father said yes, and I went with her. She clothed and fed me, and I did chores for her. At sixteen I didn't want to work for her anymore. I was with her for a year and a half, but she got fed up with me because, instead of going to rosary, I went out with my boyfriend, so she sent me back to my father.

After a few years I went to work in the house of a lady in the center of Colima when the couple went to speak with my father. I lasted there for several months. My sister worked in the same house; she did the heavier work while I cared for the three children. They paid me seventy-five pesos [U.S.$6.00], which was all for me because my brothers were caring for my father. Every week my sister and I went to visit my father.

I didn't want to be in a relationship with the man who became the father of my children because he drank. He drove a truck and went all over the country, which I also didn't like. I would break off with him and get involved with men of a better type, but he would return every so often and pick a fight with them. He wouldn't leave me alone. One day I quit my job and went away with him, and on the third day we got married. After a while I had my first daughter, but we always got into arguments, then he would get drunk, and I couldn't talk to anyone in my family about it. They just threw it back in my face because they had never approved of my marriage.

Two months after my daughter was born I went to see my father because my husband tried to beat me. I asked my father's pardon and stayed with him for eight months. Then my father spoke with the priest and they returned with me to my husband. We got along well for a time and I became pregnant with my son. I had to indulge my husband and go with him to a hamlet where he got a

job. I went with my daughter, pregnant with my son. I lasted only
for a few months there, then I returned to Colima to have my son.

A year and a half later my third child, a girl, was born, and that
was when I had the worst problems with my husband. He beat me
up badly and I left for good. I wrote to a cousin whom I had not
seen in twenty years, and I went to live with her in Tepic. I went
with only my eldest daughter because my husband took the other
two away from me. My baby daughter was only ten months old.

My cousin helped me recover from the beating and I got back on
my feet. I went to work with her, but always with the terrible pain
of not having my children with me. We cooked meals for five
engineers, but with my help we could handle more people, and at
times we fed up to twenty. The work was difficult because it
involved not only cooking, but also washing, ironing, and cleaning
their houses at times.

After living with my cousin for a while, the work started to
weigh on me. At the beginning, my relationship with her was good,
but then the arrangement deteriorated. Although I helped her and
gave her everything I earned, when she got into a bad mood she
really made my life miserable, often to the point of tears.

Among the people we cooked for was an engineer for the National Railroads; I had a good relationship with him and he was
very respectful. We knew each other for three years and he always
addressed me using the formal *"usted."* Then I had a daughter with
him.

When I told the engineer that I was pregnant, he told me a
number of things, including the fact that he had a lover. But, he
said, if I wanted to marry him and go live with him, I would never
want for anything.

When I told my cousin what the engineer had proposed to me,
she said, "If you want to leave, take your daughter and everything
and go. I can find somebody else to help me. But think it through
carefully and don't do anything you'll regret."

My daughter didn't care for the engineer and didn't want to go.
She preferred to remain with her aunt. Everything was very difficult: if I went with him I would be left without any of my children.
I couldn't make up my mind, so I stayed with my cousin, but my
belly was growing by the day and I felt very ashamed. Fortunately,
my cousin was changing, and every day she treated me better. I
worked harder than ever during those months so my cousin
wouldn't throw me out of the house.

Every day the engineers brought more of their friends, and I had
to be organized in order to feed more people. Even in this I calcu-

lated well, because there were never leftovers.

As my pregnancy became more evident, the engineer helped me financially; I never asked him for anything. I was ashamed and I worried that my family would find out back in Colima. My situation made me very anxious!

The other engineers who came to eat were delighted. They all said, "A girl! Let's hope it's a girl!" These guys didn't care for the other engineer, not because I was carrying his child, but because he was so cold and severe. During all the years they ate together, he never said more than "Good afternoon."

While I was pregnant I went only twice to the doctor, because my cousin took me, not because I was feeling bad. The doctor gave me vitamins because I was so malnourished and tired out from so much work. Besides that, I slept on the floor with my daughter, and my whole body was affected by the cold.

Two months before my daughter's birth, the engineer took me to Guadalajara for a day to buy everything the baby was going to need. I bought her little shoes, clothing, and even a bassinet, everything of the best quality. I think I was pretty demanding because I bought a lot.

The day my daughter was born the engineer wasn't there; a friend informed him and that same afternoon he returned to Tepic and came to see me. He had given me money to pay for everything three days before leaving town.

The engineer's lover couldn't have children and she wanted me to give her my daughter, she wanted to buy her. Of course I said no, but I was really shocked by the fact that she wanted to steal my child from me.

A few days after my daughter's birth I met a close friend of my cousin. This woman lived in the United States and she suggested that I go with her to work there. The woman's name was Bertha, and she told me that she could get me across to the other side.

I told my cousin that I liked the idea, but that I had to make some money in order to be able to go. The same day that Bertha was going, one of the engineers arrived and paid me five hundred pesos [U.S.$40.00]. As was customary, every two weeks almost everyone paid me, which enabled me to net some two thousand pesos [U.S.$160.00].

That same day, another engineer, one I liked a lot, said that, if I married him, he would adopt all my children. I told him no, although he really loved my daughters; he always called them "my little daughters" and brought them shoes and clothing every two weeks.

All the engineers were kind in that way. They all addressed the small one as "my daughter," and they all bought things for my girls, so that it seemed like they had many fathers.

When I told them all that I was going to Tijuana, to try to cross over to the other side—after they had paid me—they argued and insisted that I not leave. "No, skinny, don't go. You're one of us. We care about you, and without you who's going to attend to us? If you like, we'll give you more money, but don't go away!"

Despite everything that the engineers said to me, my desire to make more of life, to have something to offer my children, moved me to go with Bertha and leave my daughters with my cousin. The decision was really tough because I had to leave my newborn daughter.

So I went with Bertha. We went by road to Mexicali. I remember very well that we left at five in the morning and that I didn't eat anything on the entire trip. I was hungry and I felt bad. My breasts were very full and they ached; they were swollen and I had a fever.

I went without any idea of where I was going. When we arrived in the Mexicali station Bertha told me that she was going to cross over to the other side and that later she would get me across with the *polleros*. She said she would find a *coyote* for me and she gave me her telephone number and address in Los Angeles.[4] Bertha went to buy her ticket and I remained sitting in the station, crying and crying. I felt deceived and worried because I had no money, nothing more than what I had put aside for the trip.

Just then a very elegant, young-looking woman came by and asked me what was wrong. "Oh, ma'am, I am so sad!" I replied, telling her what had happened to me. First she grabbed a newspaper and made several calls to people looking for someone to work as a domestic, but all of them already had someone. She told me I should go see her sister-in-law in Tijuana, that she would surely be able to help me. She wrote down the address and telephone number on a napkin and gave me five hundred pesos [U.S.$40.00] so I could take a bus from right there to Tijuana, and then take a taxi to her house. "Don't tell the lady that I sent you, or that I gave you money, because she might take it from you." I couldn't stop thanking the woman.

When Bertha returned she asked me who the lady was, and what she wanted. I told her that it was someone I knew, and that she had given me the address of her sister-in-law. I also told Bertha that if she wanted to cross the border to go right ahead, but I was going to Tijuana.

Bertha copied down the address on another paper and that same night we left for Tijuana. We arrived at six in the morning and took a taxi to the house. I got out and Bertha didn't even wait for them to open the door; she left right away.

When the door opened a lady came out and I told her that her sister-in-law had sent me, and that she had given me this paper. The lady had no work to offer me, but she was disposed to help me out. She brought me inside, I told her my story, and all three of us started to cry, the woman Manuelita, her daughter, and I.

I was completely filthy from the trip because the milk had been dripping from my breasts. I was all sweaty because it was July and very hot, and on top of that I had a fever and was famished. They gave me a room and invited me to bathe; much later they gave me supper. They drained the milk from my breasts with a little machine and I felt better. I slept, and the next day I set out to find work. I didn't find anything, but in the meantime these people, with whom I lived, gave me money to send to my children.

They introduced me to a woman and I went to work as a servant in her house in Mexicali. After three months I returned to Tijuana and submitted my application to a maquiladora where they make cassettes. The supervisor, who was a friend of Manuelita's daughter, recommended me. All they asked for was my birth certificate and my primary school diploma, which I sent for from Colima.

Everyone back in Colima was amazed to hear that I was in Tijuana. I began working for the maquiladora, but only for three months, because they laid me off. They didn't have the necessary raw materials to keep us working.

To work in that maquiladora I had to go every day for something like a month to see how they worked, and they didn't pay me for that time. I woke up with the little girls—Manuelita's daughters—so I was used to getting up at four in the morning, with the objective of finding work. I learned by watching. The manager called me over to time how long it took me to assemble a cassette. In two minutes I put together three, which I was able to do because I had practiced. I started working in November 1970, and in January 1971 they laid me off. They gave me a paper saying that my layoff wasn't permanent, only temporary, due to a lack of raw materials. They left it that they would call me back in two or three months.

After three months I went back to ask for work at the same factory, and as they did have a need, I stayed to work that very same day. They gave me my reentry payment, and I've been working right up to the present [1982].

At first I was very afraid that they would lay people off again, and because I was one of the newest employees, I would be among the first to go. But fortunately that wasn't the case, because I've been working here now for twelve years and they haven't laid me off.

After working for a year they gave me a permanent contract, so I decided to rent my own room and not be a bother to Manuelita any more. In my little room I had a stove, my refrigerator, and two second-hand beds, so I went to get my daughters. I brought the elder one only during her primary school vacation. After just a few days with me in Tijuana the girl refused to eat, and she didn't want to do anything. The doctor said she missed her sister, and if I didn't bring the younger one, my elder daughter would die. I went to my boss to ask permission and returned for the younger girl, but my cousin didn't want to give her to me. She said that the girl was hers and that she had taken care of her. My little girl said to my cousin, "Mama, tell this lady to go away." Because she had always lived with my cousin, she didn't care for me.

I came back to Tijuana for the receipts and money orders to prove that I had always provided economic support for my daughter. My cousin finally gave me my daughter, who never stopped crying during the entire trip. People thought that I had kidnapped her. Once in Tijuana she got dehydrated and I had her in the hospital for two days. I continued working and my elder daughter took care of her sister.

Manuelita helped me a lot, and she's like a grandmother to my daughters. Thanks to her, my life has changed. Here I have a roof over my head, food, and money to buy clothes; before, I had nothing. This has been an advancement in my life, most of all in economic terms. And when the manager told me that I had a permanent position, I felt secure and content because I could bring my girls to live with me.

For Ángela, as for many women from nonindustrialized areas, maquiladora work represents an advance on the social scale. She could never have had a house, a washing machine, and the material goods that working on the northern border enables one to have. Working women along the northern border can acquire goods, both new and second-hand, at lower prices than elsewhere in the country. This change in their way of life is even more striking for those who migrate from rural areas.

Ángela was very grateful for the opportunity to work. The owners understand and take advantage of this gratitude in order to preserve the high productivity and quality of work, characteristics that Ángela and the other migrants possess. Recall Ángela's first words as she recounted her life: "It might seem like I exaggerate, but it gave me a great sense of happiness to start working at the maquiladora; I thought I had overcome my past. It was the moment in which God heard my prayers and changed my life."

Ángela's life in the maquiladora, like that of the majority of workers in this industry, confers conditions of privilege when compared with her past life. For her, this plant represented the opportunity to acquire a certain social status, which gave her access to consumer goods. A good part of her security came from the stable salary, which permitted her a higher degree of mobility than she had before coming to work in this factory. Ángela continued:

My life is something else; I have my house and my things, which I have bought little by little. I have bought almost everything on installment or in second-hand stores. I have worked for a number of years in the maquiladora, and I have always had the ambition to go work on the other side, find a good job, and—why not?—get married there to a good man. I think I can achieve that because various opportunities with good men have come my way. I've had a variety of pen-pal friendships with Americans. I was in the North American Club, which sent me a bulletin with addresses of people who want to meet Mexican women. It's the Club Latino of Chula Vista, California. There you can get addresses of single men. Those I've written to have replied. One was a German who lived in New York and wanted to come and marry me. We corresponded for six months and the letters were very intense. In them he recounted his entire life, and I mine. At the very moment he decided to come, I didn't want him to. He was a widower, he had a six-year-old daughter and worked in the German Consulate in New York.

I think a partnership would solve a lot of my problems. Besides, family life is very important for the couple and the children. I really like to work in the home; here I'm happy.

I'm very happy because six months ago my other two children came, the two their father had taken away from me. My son is a man of nineteen, and my daughter is sixteen. She stayed with me and the boy went to work with some uncles on the other side.

These two kids used to hate me. Their father poisoned them against me. He told them I was a prostitute, and only about seven months ago did they realize it wasn't so. Now they think their father behaved badly, that he doesn't deserve to be their father, nor did he deserve me.

I'm very pleased to have my children near me and to see them happy. The oldest daughter is now married to a good young man; they make a very attractive couple, and soon I'm going to be a grandmother.

My daughter, the sixteen-year-old, is working in another

maquiladora, an electronics plant. I would have preferred that she continue studying, but either work or study. You cannot do both at once. This girl worries me. I don't want her to lack what I have lacked, I don't want her to suffer, I don't want her to repeat history.

Obdulia

The economic situation in my home was never good, but my father was always willing to pay all the expenses the school authorities asked of us. Many of my brothers didn't wish to study. They went to work after the third year of school.

In my family there were twelve brothers and sisters, one of whom died shortly after birth. We're all the offspring of the same mother, but not the same father, because my mother married two times. I hardly have anything to do with five of my siblings because they live on the other side and they were hardly ever with us. Those of us who live here get along well, and we've always helped each other out. My eldest sister, of those of us who live on this side, is twenty-two years old. She's married and works at home. Next is my brother, who is twenty and works assembling speedometers for trailers. My younger sister is sixteen, and she is also married. She's the one who takes care of my son while I work.

I am seventeen and my son is fifteen months old. Before I got married, my sisters and I spent our time cleaning the house, which had three rooms, and washing all my brothers' clothes. My brothers didn't have to do anything around the house, even when they weren't working.

All of us who live in Tijuana were born here, and we've never gone to the other side. I don't even know the towns of Rosarito or Tecate. My parents are from Nayarit, and they came here in search of work. In the beginning my father worked as a stevedore in a market. Now he's a taxi driver and things are going much better for him. I really would like to know the land where my parents are from. If I had a little money I would go visit relatives my parents left behind. I don't know them, but if I told them I was coming, I think they would welcome me.

As long as I can remember, there have been maquiladoras in Tijuana. I think they offer good jobs there. You can earn more working there than as a domestic. Things are difficult because if you didn't study, the only thing you can do is work as a domestic. Before, even without finishing primary school, we could get a job in the factories because they didn't have so many requirements. Every day they get more demanding!

I've been working in a maquiladora for the last eight months. I was able to get a job because before there wasn't a certificate requirement like there is now. We could get a job without the primary school diploma. They just gave us a three-hour test to see how fast we could work. Now you're required to do some math problems and present a diploma. I was already married when I went to work; I saw that the other girls earned their money, bought their things, and did what they wanted. I wanted to be like them.

Before I got married I had already worked. When I was thirteen years old, I began working as a domestic. I worked there for five months; I remember that they paid me five hundred pesos [U.S.$40.00] per week. I liked the work because I got along well with the mistress of the house. Besides the household chores, I had to care for her two children. That was the most difficult. You have to have a lot of patience with children. At that time I started to feel like I wanted to go back to school; I had the desire to learn. I went back to school but after two weeks I had to get out, I couldn't make it. I wasn't born to study!

I was still thirteen when I began to work with my sister in a cookie factory. At first they didn't know my age, but when they found out they dismissed me. But my sister kept on working. We packed cookies and we put the label on the box. They paid us very little, and half of that we had to give to my mother; the other half we spent on clothing. Almost all the girls we worked with spent their money on clothing. Almost none of us had children we had to support and educate.

I liked factory work. I concerned myself with meeting more people and earning my money. Since I wasn't allowed to keep working there, I returned to school, but I went to the Social Security school. There I met Martín and started going with him. I was still a bit short of my fourteenth birthday! Everyone got very angry at home. Now they didn't want to see me.

Martín worked in a car wash and lived with his friends. When I went with him I had to live with his friends. After a while, at home they started to worry a lot about me. One day Martín's mother came and told me to go back to my parents and talk with them. I spoke with my mother, she pardoned me, and I went back to visiting them.

One time a friend told us that if we crossed to the other side we would be able to get better jobs, and one day we went with him. I remember that we crossed at night and we ran a long way, but that same day Immigration pulled us off the bus. I remember being really scared. They asked for our papers and, since we didn't have any, they pulled us off, took us away, and locked us up in some little rooms. They took me out at one in the morning, but poor Martín didn't get out until 6:00 A.M. In a van they left us in a row together with another woman who also had been grabbed. I sat with her the entire night in the center, waiting for them to let Martín out.

We've never tried to cross over again. After a year together I became pregnant with my son, and that was when we got married so we could get Social Security benefits. At that time things were going badly for us; life became more difficult than it had been. At times we didn't eat anything all day because it was the rainy season and nobody brought their cars in to be washed. Martín wasn't salaried, he earned according to the number of cars he washed. Once we went two days without eating, and we went to my mother's house to get something to eat. In exchange, Martín washed down the entire patio.

Nor did we have anywhere to sleep; we slept on the floor. For the little room where we were living we had to pay five hundred pesos [U.S.$40.00] in rent. Over time things have gotten better. Now Martín works cleaning an office and we never lack for food. We moved to this little room where we are now. It's nicer than where we were before. Be that as it may, now we have a bed and a cooking stove.

Every so often I ask myself how long I will continue to work in the maquiladora. I think I'm going to be here as long as I can, until they run me off! We all want to continue working here, as we're all used to earning our pittance. We're all afraid that they're going to dismiss us for whatever reason.

Obdulia was quiet, pensive for a moment. Then she concluded:

I hope that my son is successful in his studies and becomes a doctor. He's been at it for a year and a half, and I'm going to help him so he can continue. Being a doctor must be an excellent career; anyway it's better to work on your own account than to be under a supervisor's thumb all day long.

María Cristina

I was born in Guadalajara in 1959. At that time Mama devoted herself to the household and my father was a journalist. When I was about five months old we came to live in Baja California. We came because people said that it was better here.

Actually, everything went well for us, and now my father is a printer; he's the owner of a print shop. At first he was an employee in Ensenada. He went there first by himself, and later brought us and my mother. Sometimes he wrote articles for a newspaper, but he wasn't satisfied because he didn't earn enough, so he went away to the other side. He stayed there for four or five years assembling heavy equipment. Meanwhile, we kept on living in Ensenada in our own house. My father got tired of working on the other side and returned to Ensenada to work. Then he got tired of his work and came to Tijuana. Because the daily commute between Ensenada and Tijuana was very tiring he brought us here. They sold the house in Ensenada and we rented one here.

Altogether we are nine brothers and sisters plus my parents. That's why my father had to look for work in order to support us all. I'm the eldest sister. I went to primary school in Ensenada, and I was quite happy there. I didn't want to come here; I remember that when we did, I cried a lot. I was thirteen when we came. Here in Tijuana I no longer wanted to study. It wasn't because my parents couldn't pay that I didn't go to secondary school, but just because I was lazy. I didn't like it anymore. My younger siblings have gone on in school; some are still studying, and others are working.

We all get along well. The next sister after me works with my father in the printing plant; she has a daughter and is a single mother. After her comes my brother, who works in a brewery. Next comes another brother, who also works in the print shop with my father. Next comes Blanca, who is twenty-eight; she also works with my father, but she is married. After her come four more brothers who don't work because they're much younger, all in primary school.

At home the women all help when my mother needs it. But now I get home from work and take it easy because in the afternoon there are no chores. I've been working some four years now, and before that I helped my father in the print shop. But I didn't like working there. At the shop, my father values my brother's work more; he hardly paid us girls anything, only my brother. So I decided to leave, because I couldn't take working there anymore. I worked a lot and hardly made anything, even though I was a secretary.

I never went out for fun; I was always shut away in the house, not because they didn't give me permission, but just because I like being a homebody. I didn't like going out because I've always been very shy. But now that I'm working I've changed a lot, in my attitudes and my way of thinking.

Before, I didn't pay any attention to my appearance; I wasn't interested in looking good. I had never had a boyfriend; my life didn't revolve around going out with anyone. I just always stayed at home, slovenly and unkempt; I never brushed my hair or bathed. But time went by and my sister got pregnant, which made me think about a lot of things.

When I started working at the factory I got to know a lot of guys and girls. Now on Fridays I go downtown with my boyfriend at one in the afternoon, and get home around nine o'clock. There's a lot to do downtown. We walk around, have something to eat, go to the park, see a movie, and that's how we spend our time. My boyfriend pays for everything, and he won't let me pay for anything.

From the 2,548 pesos [U.S.$45.00] that I make per week, I contribute 700 [U.S.$12.00] to the household. With the rest I buy clothing, makeup, and cosmetics for myself and put money aside for bus fare, my meals, and anything else I might want to buy.

Alma

I went to primary school until sixth grade, then my father sacrificed to buy me a sewing machine. I don't have a certificate, but for a year and a half I learned how to use it from some women who were very good seamstresses. I watched how they cut fabric, how they attached a collar, and that's how I learned. It was a private house, not a school or academy, nothing like that. I stopped learning sewing because I had to get married, and then I didn't continue. But in my house, with the little I'd learned, I made clothes for my children.

I was born in the State of Oaxaca, in a village called Cacahuatepec, very close to Guerrero. The village is very pretty; there's a lot of vegetation, and the temperature is very agreeable, not like here, where in the cold season it's very cold, and in the hot season it's very hot. I grew up there in Cacahuatepec and got married there. When I came to Tijuana ten years ago I was thirty-two years old. Seeing that I wasn't making enough to live on, I wrote to a sister-in-law who lived here and invited her to visit us there. For some time she had been urging us to come to Tijuana, where perhaps we could make a life for ourselves. But my husband never had wanted to leave. That time, though, I took it into my head to go, and I told him, "Well, I'm going, even if you don't. I'm going because I'm tired of life here, and I'm taking all my children so there won't be a quarrel, and so you can't say that I'm leaving you tied down, nothing like that. I'm taking them all. If you want to follow, let's go. If not, then stay here and bring in the harvest"—he already had a crop in—"and sell it. With that money you can come if you want to leave here."

He devoted himself to the land. He had a small parcel that he had purchased where he planted beans and corn. What we harvested was scarcely enough to eat; the land didn't produce much because it's so worn out. So we came to Tijuana. At that point in the village I was just so desperate because I saw how much I worked to produce nothing; there was no return on what we put into it, hardly enough to get by, and my children were eating badly.

We had seven children plus the two of us, nine in all, and we all came. My husband didn't study past second grade; he knows nothing, except that he can write and sign his name. Here he works in construction as a mason. My oldest daughter is twenty-two, and she's a nurse. She had two years of secondary schooling in Mexico City with one of my husband's brothers, but she wrote that she didn't have enough money, at times not even enough for her books and the notebooks she needed. Sometimes we sent her money, but not always.

My next daughter is twenty; she studied in CONALEP[5] as a production technician, in a course that follows secondary school. She also works in an electronics maquiladora. After her is the eldest boy, who is eighteen. He's finishing secondary school, and started a job washing cars yesterday. He got up very early this morning and left; we'll see how it goes for him.

I have another son, sixteen, who's beginning secondary school. After him comes Abad, fourteen, who's in fourth grade. Then comes his twelve-year-old brother and the ten-year-old girl; both of them are in third grade. And last is the youngest boy, six years old, who is finishing kindergarten.

I started working when we got here. My first job was to work in a household. That was about ten years ago, and I earned fifteen dollars, which was a lot. It was enough to meet expenses. I left that job after two months because my sister-in-law arrived, and she told us that we should go to the other side, so we did. We were there for two years, and during that time my husband worked only four months, and that right at the end. But with the money we made we returned. We had five kids with us where we lived, in Long Beach, which is part of Los Angeles. There I worked in a very small clothing maquiladora with about ten employees; I lasted for about eight months. I earned around thirty-five dollars, and when things went especially well for me, I made forty dollars. The owners were

Cubans; they were good but they paid very badly. They paid us by the piece. They liked to hire undocumented workers, because that way they didn't have to pay what they should have. They gave us nothing, no insurance, no vacations, nothing.

So I changed to another maquiladora. My nephews helped me get that job, because they speak English very well. They took me there, spoke with the manager, who said he was going to hire me provisionally for a week. If I could do it, I could stay, which I did, because I met the quota they expected of me. That maquiladora was bigger; it had about sixty employees. I took home eighty dollars there, and that was enough for us to leave my sister-in-law's house and pay rent, because they say that the dead man and the guest begin to stink after three days. So we had to leave.

In the second maquiladora I lasted for a year and a half. The majority of us were Mexican women. That company didn't provide insurance either; they didn't give anything in the way of benefits. In the majority of the factories over there, as in the Tijuana maquiladoras, they don't hire men, only women.

While we were there, my sister-in-law succeeded in enrolling my children in school. They took classes in English, and they were more or less learning the language. There my daughter reached sixth grade, and it was a lot of work for her. She was promoted to secondary school just because she got the highest math score in the entire school. When we returned here, those two years counted for nothing. They only served to help her learn English.

There I paid $150 in rent. It was a lot but I managed it. I paid for everything—electricity, water, rent, and food—and I was still sending money to my son who had stayed in Tijuana to study. He stayed with an aunt, his father's sister.

Because I was working all day on the other side, I didn't become aware of the problems that young people have living in the United States. Because my husband was at home all day, he saw the problems and he complained at every opportunity, saying he didn't want to live there. He was always telling me we should return to Tijuana. When he told me what was happening with the kids, I was surprised, but I thought I would never be able to earn as much as in the United States, because they paid less in Tijuana.

But we couldn't return to Tijuana because we didn't have any money saved, and for that we needed money, at least enough to pay everyone's return passage. Besides, because I was established there and was making good money, the truth is I never really pushed myself to come back. Sometimes I managed to earn $115 a week. It was enough for all our needs, but of course everything was a lot cheaper than now.

My children resented going to live over there. They had to speak another language and the customs are very different. But because I listened to my sister-in-law, I brought them along. We went to the United States out of hunger. She took the kids across as her own in her car, and we crossed under the barbed wire. And very quickly Immigration grabbed us and deported us.

My sister-in-law paid for our trip from Oaxaca and the "service" for getting us across, and she also endured our presence in her house for a good while. She helped us out a lot.

One time when I left work, Immigration grabbed me. My sister-in-law was thinking that my youngest daughter could become the way to secure residency. She baptized my daughter there and by means of those papers we might have stayed there, but I didn't speak English. I was working all day long, and in order to arrange those papers you have to hustle from one place to another, because it's like in Mexico; they charge us wherever we turn.

The truth is that there are a lot of conveniences there, and the houses you rent are prettier and bigger. The only thing we had were some beds that someone had given us. When we got the money together to return to Tijuana we came, and for the first week we stayed with another of my husband's sisters. Then we rented a little room for everyone.

My husband went to the South to arrange the sale of a house that he had in Oaxaca, and I found work. He stayed for three months and couldn't sell the house. The work I got was in a clothing maquiladora. I was pregnant at the time but they needed workers, and because they saw that I could sew very well, they didn't do a medical exam and hired me. I worked there for six years, and I was about thirty-six when I started there.

Tijuana is full of people from the South who want to cross over to the other side because you earn in dollars. But all that glitters is not gold: it's true that you are paid in dollars, but you also spend in dollars. So it comes to the same thing. Here the dollar is worth something, but not over there, because everything is very expensive. The conveniences are the only good thing about the other side.

If I were to compare the jobs there and those here, I'd say that it comes to the same thing. Here we earn less than on the other side but rents here are much lower. At the moment I'm paying seven hundred pesos [U.S.$25.92 in January 1982, $4.80 in December] a month for this little room.

Working conditions were better on the other side, but not much. There we had air conditioning and heat, but in the Mexican factory there is nothing like that. The only thing they do for us is bring in a fan when it's hot so we don't bake, but when it's cold you have to go to work bundled up if you're going to keep from freezing. They also put in some little ovens so we can warm our food.

I think my life has changed since I began working in the maquiladora. I can't deny it because I was killing myself back in Oaxaca working to get somewhere. By contrast, although it's the same situation here, at least my kids eat pretty well, there's food on the table, and they've had the opportunity to study. Back home we never drank milk, much less ate meat, mostly because we didn't have enough money.

But sometimes, even though we had money, we couldn't get the food we needed. There where we lived there wasn't much from the outside in the way of food. Also it's difficult to find a doctor there, and if one of my kids got sick, I had a hell of a time curing them. Not only do I think my life has changed, but also I can say that it has improved. Yes, the outcome has been good from having come here, despite the sacrifices we have made. I'm certain that if we had stayed in the village, my children would not have studied, because your income there doesn't allow for anything more than survival.

One of the factors that distinguish Alma, Ángela, María Luisa, and thousands of other women is their place of origin. They are the product of socioeconomic conditions that are so distinct, so minimal in terms of development indicators, that when they arrive in the cities of the North it leaves an imprint on their lives and attitudes. The minimal transportation and communications infrastructure in the original communities impedes local populations' ability to migrate. Likewise, it constricts their access to consumer goods, both durable and perishable, as well as to a range of urban services and infrastructural advantages that are severely limited in their places of origin.

Now they live in a city whose cosmopolitan character offers access to a great variety of products from many countries. They engage in an exchange of ideas with people from other regions, and their relationships include contact with North Americans, Japanese, and Middle Easterners, among other foreigners. They learn about migration and become familiar with their surroundings, acclimating to a social space and to conditions of everyday life that they never imagined existed.

It should be remembered that Tijuana borders on California, one of the richest states in the United States. The United States is the premier capitalist power and presents itself as the nation that offers unlimited access and possibilities. It is instructive to consider the radical cultural and economic changes that maquiladora workers have undergone, as so vividly elucidated in the testimonies of Ángela, María Luisa, and Alma. In mundane terms they expressed their change experience as "having won the lottery" or as a stroke of good luck.

Analyzing their testimonies enables us to see how, for the majority of the migrants, moving to Tijuana and working in a maquiladora has produced changes in the composition of the domestic group (as in Ángela's case), in the division of labor, in cultural patterns, and so forth. This becomes even more evident in the case of female migrants from rural to urban zones.

These women foresaw a well-defined future in their places of origin. A woman had to prepare herself diligently for marriage and the role of the exemplary wife. Her activities in the village were circumscribed by the tasks of the home. She had to be completely prepared to attend to male household members when they returned from work. Her task was to prepare them to return to work the next day.

In María Luisa's commentary we can see how she and her sisters were expected to help their mother with household chores: grinding corn, carrying water, and taking care of the animals. Ángela's responsibilities were not much different; her job was to care for the pigs and chickens, to carry water, and to help sell eggs. For all of the women it was very clear that, had they remained, they never would have been able to liberate themselves from domestic slavery, from the responsibilities enforced by motherhood, economic dependence on their husbands, or, much less, to secure political rights. There was nothing to hope for, and there was no other way to conceive of the world besides living under outright oppression.

Coming to work in the maquiladoras presents a new perspective predicated on economic independence. For capital, it is profitable to utilize women in this type of industry, but it is necessary that these women also fulfill their prescribed domestic function.

To work in the maquiladora alters to some extent a woman's idea of the future, her presumed vocation and appointed destiny. Her range of options widens, and her daily activities, in the beginning, appear to be enriched. Women who enter the realm of productive activity encounter five social relations that are integral to women's oppression: social labor, domestic labor, children, family, and sexuality (Broyelle 1975).

The latter four social relations have already been considered, but social labor is a new experience for the majority of the maquiladora workers. As already seen, for 52 percent of the interviewees this represents their first labor experience. It poses the opportunity to recognize that they have common interests as women and as a socioeconomic class. This recognition is fundamental in resolving the question of individual identity.

On the other hand, as Ángela and Alma noted, working in Tijuana enabled their children to pursue their studies beyond the primary-school level. For the mother, employment in the maquiladora became a categorical index of her violent integration into a distinct realm of labor experience, although in many cases, perhaps the majority, the sons and daughters of the maquiladora workers are not, and will not become, workers in these industries. A return to their places of origin had little attraction for these women, despite the unyielding working conditions of the maquiladora and the assault on human dignity these conditions represent. To be able to count on a regular income sufficient to meet their minimum economic necessities was an important factor, one highly relevant in any consideration of whether to return to their place of origin.

Massive changes are evident in each of these women's stories, in the mutable circumstances of their past and present lives. These changes inform their attitudes toward their condition as workers today. They had no history or experience of worker consciousness, and hence no commitment vis-à-vis their situation as laborers that might enable them to interact like those born into a working-class environment and conditioned by that social fact. In the manner of Simone de Beauvoir,[6] we might say that these women are not born as workers, but they become workers insofar as they understand their status as workers in the maquiladora plants to be a merely transitory condition. Many maquiladora workers think that, just as they have been able to achieve "a better life," perhaps—as Ángela said—they can arrange to marry a U.S. citizen and thus be able to live in the United States and enjoy all the associated conveniences. In her commentary Ángela revealed the prevailing idealization of life in the United States.

The working women of the maquiladoras, even when they have worked for many years in the same plant, generally have a very short career. Having experienced economic independence, however, they will find it difficult to accept the social implications of ending their careers.

What happens to those women who, for reasons of occupational disability, the loss of manual dexterity, or family pressures, find themselves obliged to stop working? What has become of the thousands of displaced workers, those laid-off women who once saw in the maquiladora the only viable means to become part of the productive workforce? These are some of the questions that remain to be answered.

Notes

1. Form 13 is a legal document granted by the secretary of home affairs to confirm the holder's residence in the border region. To qualify, one must have resided at least six months in a northern Mexican frontier district. Form 13 is essential to enter the United States on a temporary basis; U.S. immigration authorities require it to extend what is commonly known as a "local passport," or "border-crossing card."

2. The Cristero Rebellion (1926–1929) climaxed a century of animosity between the Catholic Church and the Mexican state. Following the 1910 revolution, the revolutionaries tried to impose severe limitations on the church. When in 1926 the government decreed strict enforcement of anticlerical legislation, Catholics all over the country took up arms. The warfare continued until a settlement was reached in 1929, when the government agreed to allow the church to perform its spiritual offices under its own internal discipline.

3. It is uncertain to which general she refers. It could be Enrique Gorostieta, leader of the *cristero* movement in Jalisco. In 1928 he was named Chief of the National Liberation Army.

4. A *pollero* is, literally, a person who tends chickens. In this case, however, a *pollero* is an entrepreneur who lives by taking advantage of people who, because they are inexperienced and in the unfamiliar and potentially dangerous situation of wanting to enter the United States illegally, must depend on the *pollero*. The *pollero* contracts to get them across the border undetected. The allusion is to the unenviable fate of the domesticated fowl. Similarly, a coyote, like the animal namesake in popular folklore, is a trickster, a crafty and often unscrupulous individual who agrees to transport the undocumented across the border, but with no guarantees.

5. CONALEP, Consejo Nacional de Educación Profesional (National Professional Education Council), part of the Secretaría de Educación Pública (Public Education Ministry), exists in all Mexican states and offers training for technical careers.

6. *El segundo sexo*, p. 13. DeBeauvior's original idea was that women are born female, biologically speaking, but they have to *learn* to be female in a social sense.

6.

Most Beautiful Flower
of the Maquiladora

One time, about five years ago, a girl from the factory competed to become "Queen of the Maquiladora." Many girls participated from almost all the factories. I think the fiesta was organized by the governor. Each factory selected its representative, and looks were what was important. The most beautiful girl was the winner.

María Luisa continued:

Every so often we have a fiesta in the plant. We have an annual party; you might say that we celebrate the factory's birthday. The owners bring in food and they gives us a half day off. We stop work at noon; they bring out the food and put on some music. Then we all chat and the managers are very laid back. They also give fiestas for us on Christmas, Halloween, and Easter, and some girls exchange gifts on those dates.

Marta—a young woman of sixteen who, in addition to working, attended secondary school—commented:

In our case, every year the owners arrange a trip for us to Ensenada, and they pay for everything. Every two weeks they make barbecue, paid for by the manager. They also organize volleyball and basketball championships for us, and some of the girls compete against other factories. I came to work in this factory because my friend Lety told me they treated her very well, and that they also help her to continue studying.

Marta said proudly:

When you come to work in this factory, they give classes about the work we're going to do. They test us to see if we understand, and they pay us for the entire training period. On top of that, they give us a specified amount of money every month as a bonus, but only if we have not been late or absent from work, and have taken no excused absences.

Marta (María Luisa's niece) commented with considerable emotion:

All of us who work in these factories are quite young, and the supervisors worry about us as if they were our parents. They're always hurrying us up so we don't get to class late, because the majority of us who work there also go to school.

The maquiladoras sponsor a variety of recreational and athletic activities, including parties, dances, dinners, raffles, beauty pageants, walks, country outings, and sports events. These activities distract the workers and occupy their attention during a good part of their free time. To some extent this keeps them from reflecting on their exploitation as workers and their oppression as women while minimizing the antagonistic character of relations between worker and boss.

I do not mean to represent these recreational and sports activities as negative in themselves. The maquiladoras utilize these naturally healthful activities, however, to achieve a precise ideological objective: to distract, inhibit, and prevent reflection; to arrest the development of any attitude that might endanger productivity. As in all corporate-sponsored extracurricular activities, the firms rationalize the beauty pageants as "recreational" pursuits. They are, however, intended to help boost productivity and, by reaffirming traditional standards of feminine beauty and behavior, convey to the female worker the firm's profound preoccupation with her physical and emotional well-being. These events reflect an intention to reaffirm women's subordination by promoting mildness, submission, and passivity and by playing on the women's capacity for emotion.

The ideological control mechanisms that prevail inside the maquiladoras are profoundly sexist. Attitudes of male superiority embrace all spheres of productive life and the social relations in the factory. Such attitudes are expressed in their superiors' paternalistic treatment of female workers; their superiors are nearly always men. The ideology of female inferiority is manifest in the prevailing division of labor in the maquiladoras. Women are charged with tasks that are delicate and monotonous, work seen as requiring considerable patience and dexterity. Men assume responsibility for activities requiring action and endurance and for those things requiring reason and leadership.

Marta commented matter-of-factly:

The supervisor takes to flirting with me, saying, "You're the best worker, and that's why you're my favorite." Soon all the women are jealous because he treats me better than them, and they all stop talking to me. After several days he says the same thing to another, and all the women get jealous again. We are always competing to be the best and become the favorite. Every day the girls go to work more and more decked out, and no sooner do we complain about something we don't like than the bosses tell us, "Arguing is not ladylike; if you get angry it makes you unattractive, and then we won't be fond of you."

Women in the factories are daily treated as sexual objects, which negates their individual integrity while reproducing and reinforcing a sexist ideology. To some degree such treatment is contradictory in that women are urged to present themselves as sexual objects in order to preserve their employment and their position within the labor hierarchy. As various bosses have put it, "Girls, utilize your sexuality." Hence, struggling to be liked by the boss, to become his pet, becomes an obligatory habit and daily purpose if one wants to survive in the workplace.

But if feminine sexuality is encouraged in the maquiladora, it is simultaneously repressed. Active sexual agency is specified as a male prerogative whose sole objective is reproduction. According to Wilhelm Reich, sexual repression is useful to capital because it is transformed, by means of sublimation, into a capacity for labor. This would explain the capacity of the woman, inconceivable in a man, to simultaneously assume all the responsibilities of her gender in a patriarchal society and at the same time to be efficient in the workplace (in Sau 1981:190).

Ángela said:

I don't get along well with the boss; I don't even speak to him. Some women do get along with him, but they don't respect him. Many bosses have lovers from the plant. My own factory chief, the one who authorizes the permits to go to Social Security, has a lover in the factory, even though he's married and has two daughters. Everybody knows it, because he's also had affairs with other girls there. There are thousands of cases like this in the factories.

Abuses result when the bosses consort with the girls. One former boss of ours had a lover who worked with me making cassettes. But now she no longer works; she lives with him and they have three children. Besides her, he goes out with other young

girls from the same place and has children with them, too. All
these girls are so young, single minors whom he has brainwashed.
That boss we had was a very coarse person, quick to paw you with
his hands. I never even said good morning to him. He was the
worst kind of person! It's an everyday thing for the bosses to invite
a girl to dinner and proceed from there, and the stupid girls acqui-
esce to see what they can get out of it: to keep their preferred shift,
to keep from being fired, or to be promoted to a supervisory position.

Marta commented:

Yes, it's true. In the factory where I work the manager had his pets.
In the beginning there was just one, then there were more. We all
knew it because we all saw it happening. His pet was an operator,
then after a while she became a supervisor. This happens a lot in
the factories, but it depends on the woman. I've only known two
cases like this, but people say it's very common.

Such testimony recalls an interesting comment a maquiladora worker
in Ciudad Juárez once made to me: "We women all believe that one way
to end our working careers is to get married, above all to someone with
a good position, like a supervisor, but I'm very concerned because there
are very few men, not enough to go around, I think." On various occasions, together with friends, she organized raffles to win a date with a
guy. Her task consisted in finding someone who was disposed to be
raffled off. They sold fifty chances for one hundred pesos [U.S.$4.30]
each, and the woman who won spent twenty-four hours with him. The
money was for the winner to pay all the expenses: food, the disco cover
charge, drinks, dinner, and the hotel.

To go out dancing, to see a film, to eat, or to have drinks with one's
girlfriends on Fridays and Saturdays are common diversions among the
younger female workers, who have fewer economic responsibilities.
When they go out they wear the latest fashions, on which they spend a
large portion of their salaries. There are many ways to induce female
workers to buy an infinity of products. Ángela commented:

When we go to work we don't go really dressed up like the youngest girls of the other factories. Where I work many women wear
skirts or dresses because their religion requires it, but others of us
prefer to wear pants. A lot of women spend money on clothes, but I
can't because my money doesn't go that far.

In some factories there is a credit arrangement with Dorians [at the time, the most prominent clothing chain in Baja California]. After working for six months in that factory they extend credit to you. There the workers buy whatever they like, as long as they don't go over a hundred dollars, and all they have to do is sign. Later they deduct it from your paycheck. The bad thing is they deduct it whenever they feel like it. Some women want them to take it out more promptly so they can get out of debt faster, and thus be able to continue buying. One friend who bought things at Christmas still hasn't been charged four months later, and because they deduct it from your check in the form of dollars, with the devaluation she's going to have to pay double. Now the dollar is at forty-seven pesos, but before it was at twenty-six. The store played stupid and took its time paying in order to make more money.

Many times vendors operate right outside the factories, but they also sell inside, even though it's prohibited. There was one girl, another factory worker, who came with her bag full of dresses and boxes of shoes, and the girls went into the bathrooms to try on everything she brought. Because a lot of women would stop working to go see the merchandise, one time the supervisors instituted a search of all our bags. Even so, every so often a vendor slips in with some blouses to sell.

Furniture makers also solicit outside the maquiladora and sell on credit, but that way the cost goes up a lot. They bring catalogs or furniture. There is also an abundance of women selling products from Avon and Standhome. What can I say? We all try to struggle to make some extra change. So we walk out of the factory having spent everything; when they pay us we already owe our whole paychecks.

Also common are the women who bring back special orders from the other side, food mostly. After you get to know them you ask them to buy things for you, or they make themselves known by promoting their services around the plant, and that's how they get their clients. That's their business, whether they work on the other side or rely entirely on this way of making a living. Before the devaluation this was a real convenience, but now it's hardly advantageous for anything, except to buy milk—even though it's no cheaper than here, the milk is better over there. The same is true for packaged bread.

In addition to being exposed to all the alienation mechanisms implemented inside the factory, workers are also subject, like the population at large, to a barrage of values disseminated by the dominant class. These values are transmitted principally via the mass media, both Mexican and North American, to which border workers have access.

Apart from verbal messages, the mass media also transmit images of cultural practice, behavior, and material consumption. For example, television conveys attitudes, gestures, modes of behavior, ideals of physical beauty, and the like as forms to be imitated. These cultural manifestations convey habits, customs, opinions, identity, and cultural and ideological codes with which workers are unfamiliar. This cultural transmission process has as its goal the reproduction of the social system in its entirety. All these messages, from both Mexico and North America, have influenced custom and tradition, creating and reinforcing new patterns of consumption. Many female workers conform to dress and makeup fashions established by the mass media.

A broad sector of the population spends a good part of its wages on clothing and beauty products and, more generally, on a great variety of luxuries that encourage women to believe that they are less exploited or oppressed. They feel like participants in modern society when they enjoy such amenities as credit.

Two out of five female workers interviewed have to pay their debts religiously every two weeks to the furniture outlets, clothing stores, and automobile dealers. Commented Amelia:

> I scarcely get my money and I have to turn it over completely to the furniture outlet. I had to buy a bunk bed for my children, but the only way to do it was to go into debt. As long as I can remember I have had debts with half the world.

A spectrum of abiding ideological control mechanisms operates in the maquiladoras. The newsletters published by some firms demonstrate the ideological manipulation dedicated to impeding the rise of working-class consciousness. Their objective is to disseminate values opposed to those of the laboring class and to attempt to ideologically cloak the system of exploitation based on the division of labor, the salary structure, and so forth. A "Letter from the Boss" [*Carta del jefe*] in one such newsletter read:

> We undertake the same work, and follow the same schedule. We have much in common: we fight for better living conditions for those dearest to our hearts, and by means of working we strive to secure for them everything that we received—or perhaps did not receive—in our own childhood.
>
> Another reason I hold you in such high regard is that we depend on one another. Being your boss simply signifies assuming a degree

of responsibility for the work you do . . . If you do it well, my
responsibility will be fulfilled. If you do it badly, we fail together,
and I will be obliged to impose a solution.
    . . . I am your boss, but I am also your friend . . .
    . . . With regards, your boss. (*Boletín Informativo de
Electrocomponentes de México*, no. 186 [Ciudad Juárez, Chihuahua, 1980])

This policy is intended to make the worker feel as though she or he is
an important part of the enterprise, with direct responsibilities for the
firm's progress. Of course, this is true in that it is precisely the worker
who carries out production. Yet this is presented as a natural obligation.
At the same time, management's desire is to create the impression that
the firm is concerned with the worker's well-being, when what truly
matters is production. "We are all one big family. Let's unite for security,
order, and a clean plant" [poster in the Electrocomponentes de México
plant, Ciudad Juárez, Chihuahua, 1980].

Security, order, and cleanliness are fundamental to sustaining quick
and precise industrial production; they do not reflect an interest in
maintaining worker health or minimizing health and safety hazards.
And while the notion of being "one big family" ostensibly seeks to
maintain workplace harmony, it simultaneously fosters competition in
a tactic intended to boost production. Competition between workers
also has significant ideological repercussions in that the desire to
advance, and thus secure certain types of personal rewards within the
firm, divides workers, which affects their capacity for collective organization.

All these control mechanisms are furthered via messages that incul-
cate models of behavior and social relations that are integral to the daily
lives of working women. These mechanisms rely on the symbolic
manipulation of a specious ideology of feminine responsibility, at times
using moral blackmail to further productivity and reinforce the prevailing model of labor organization.

Inside the maquiladoras women have begun, in both ideology and
practice, to deploy novel approaches to the roles and values traditionally
ascribed to womankind. They are mobilizing to escape the subjugation
of a circumscribed domestic role as they contrive to realize their
liberation as competent, strong, and independent working women with
aspirations. This (from the workers' perspective) is the woman that the
factories require.

7.

Solidev:

An Embattled Maquiladora

The formation of the union and the struggles of female workers in the maquiladora Solidev Mexicana, S.A., warrant consideration in an analysis of labor movements in transnational corporations. Solidev provides an example of the international character that labor conflicts assume in this type of industry.

Solidev Mexicana, S.A., was a subsidiary of Solitron Devices, Inc. It was established in Mexico in 1969 to produce semiconductors for the Pentagon, the U.S. Department of State, International Telephone and Telegraph, and Honeywell. Solitron Devices has plants not only in Mexico, but also in the United States (San Diego, California, and Riviera Beach, Florida), England, and Germany.

The importance of Solidev's manufactured products and the magnitude of its contracts was such that by 1974, it employed 1,500 workers.[1] Over time the number of employees decreased, and by October 1982, only about 290 workers remained. The largest number of layoffs occurred in the wake of the economic crisis that arose in the United States in 1974–1975.

Solidev assumed a high profile in August 1979, when its employees founded the Solidev Independent Labor Union (Sindicato Independiente Solidev). The union won workers improved benefits, salary increases, a forty-hour work week with fifty-six hours' compensation (to offset the peso devaluation, as mandated by law), more egalitarian relations between management and workers, and greater job security. These gains vexed the Maquiladora Association [Asociación de Maquiladoras],[2] which considered Solidev a bad example.

The union distinguished itself in a struggle of more than two years to achieve better working conditions. Both state government and the private sector, however, sought to engineer the plant's closure and, despite the workers' struggle, to grant them only part of their demands.

This chapter concerns Gabriela's participation, in the formation of the Solidev union and the impact of the experience on her life. Gabriela's

Support from the people of Tijuana and from other unions helped provide a role model for Solidev.

Support for the strike came from national and international unions. Signs all over Tijuana demanded respect for workers' rights.

account provides an example of the advance organized struggle represents for the women of the maquiladoras. This chapter is not intended as a historical analysis of the union, but as a case study illustrating the social and political transformation undergone by one of its members. Gabriela observed:

> We began to organize around two problems that concerned us greatly. The first arose when they fired some of the supervisors we workers saw as sympathetic to our situation. They were good workers, good people, and even though they treated us operators strictly and always defended the owners' interests, it seemed to us that their firing was unfair. We stood up for them because, can you imagine, first the bosses were running them off, and we were going to be next. If they did that to people who were supervisors, what would they do to us? The manager wanted to pay them only for the last week they worked, plus the first week's pay, which they don't pay when you start working and hold in reserve regardless of how long you have worked in the factory. They told one of the supervisors he had wasted material valued at $15,000, but it wasn't true. It was just a pretext to fire him. Those troubles began to make us all nervous. We just couldn't let the affair go by, because the owners were going to crush us.
>
> We became concerned and began to think about what we could do. We thought about staging a work stoppage so at least they would give the fired supervisors what was owed them. We didn't have to let the owners fire us unexpectedly.
>
> Even after they were fired, the supervisors returned to the factory three days in a row, until the administrators physically threw them out of the plant. All this occurred in 1978. The manager told us that if we continued with our scheme they would fire us all. We all staged a work stoppage, except for three male workers who refused. During the work stoppage we agreed to go out on strike. It was the only way to protest the firings, and all we were asking for was that the firm give the fired supervisors what they were owed.
>
> We had become aware of a very serious problem. The manager of the factory was passing himself off as a physician. Every time a girl applied for a job, the manager told the secretaries to send the girls to him for a medical exam. He had no authority to do that because he was not a physician. Besides, as manager his only responsibility was to request the number of employees he needed. Hiring decisions, based on an aptitude test, not a medical examination, were the personnel manager's responsibility. Women said that instead of

giving them a math test involving addition and subtraction problems, he told them to lie down for an exam because he was a doctor. They had to take off their clothes and he fondled them. They say that sometimes he gave them something to drink, but he put something in it to drug them so he could violate them without their screaming.

At first, we women who worked there weren't aware of this, because he only did it with women who were looking for work, the recently arrived in Tijuana, because they couldn't complain or they were naïve, and a lot of women didn't say anything because they were embarrassed and ashamed, or because they needed work. The poor girls were sixteen or seventeen, very trusting girls. They were so innocent that they began to relate what had happened, and that's how we began to become aware of the situation. We were incensed, and we decided to throw ourselves into the struggle. It showed that they were walking all over us, they were bleeding and humiliating us, and we couldn't go on that way.

The next day, after the work stoppage, they spoke with us because by then the manager and his staff had heard that we were going to risk going out on strike. They told us repeatedly not to do it because we were going to have a lot of problems, that we would be left out on the street. They said a lot of things to us. About three days later, during work hours, they called a meeting of all personnel, and the owners were furious. They told us what could happen to us if we went out on strike. They threatened to close the plant and said we wouldn't be able to find work anywhere else, they would make sure of that. But, if we didn't strike, we could keep our jobs.

The boss kept on trying to brainwash us so we wouldn't strike. One fellow worker many of us had confidence in spoke to us about what it was to go out on strike. He told us we should really think it through because going on strike wasn't a lark; it would mean a lot of work and sacrifice.

The owner spoke to us again for about a half hour before we initiated the strike. He was really the severe type and had never spoken directly to us. But that day he spoke to everyone. He was even offering us chewing gum. By contrast, on any other day, if he saw us idle, he immediately started yelling. That day he arrived saying that he wanted to have a meeting with us inside the factory in order to talk about the strike. He told us once again that we shouldn't go on strike because we were going to lose in the end, and then we weren't going to be able to get work in another maquiladora because we'd be notorious as strikers. Our fellow worker, the one who later became our leader, told the owner it was inevitable because he had not acceded to our demands. Enraged, the boss told us if that's what we wanted to do, then go ahead, but he was going to fight tooth and nail.

We decided to go out on strike, and for all of us it was difficult and extraordinary. It seemed appealing the first few days, but then people started to get tired. I felt very uncomfortable pounding the pavement soliciting. It was unsettling; I felt very self-conscious walking around hustling for money on the street. It was difficult for me to go around selling food. But I did everything in the strike. I went out to solicit, prepared food and sold it, cared for my fellow workers' children—I helped any way I could. I also took part in the nighttime patrols to watch the plant. Everything was very well organized. Some of us did certain things while other strikers worked on other very important matters.

The strike taught me a lot of things. I confess that in the beginning I felt somehow ashamed to be on strike, but then I realized that it was really a worthy cause. We were fighting for something just, and we had nothing to be ashamed of. I never refused to take part in the strike, but I didn't always feel good doing everything we did.

When we went out vending, we sold soft drinks and food. A lot of people helped and encouraged us. They told us we should keep it up. Others called us "lazy crazies" and shouted at us, "Get back to work!" But you see, those are people with money, people with businesses whose interests were threatened by our strike. But working people like us don't say that, they always support us.

After three days we began to lose heart. It seemed like the problem wasn't going to be resolved. So we thought. At the beginning we all thought it was a game, but by the third day we realized that it was something very serious, and that things were getting more difficult by the day. We were on strike for about a month and a half, and, fortunately, we prevailed.

Because the majority of us on strike were women, a variety of problems arose with our families and acquaintances. One of the girls who worked with us has six children. Only two live with her, and the other four are with her mother, but she has to send them money. She was one of those who really joined in the strike, but she also had serious problems because she didn't have anyone to take care of her children. At the same time, her landlady wanted to run her out when she found out that our fellow worker was participating in the strike. I think the landlady must have been a friend of the factory owner. If not, how do you explain their running her out

of her house for being a striker? Well, they threw her out with all
her things! She brought her problem to the union, and we all
helped her. Another worker offered to let her and her children live
in her house. Among us we managed to help her.

The strike was very well organized. From the money we put
together we gave to those fellow workers who needed it most.
There were some who needed to pay their rent, because if they
didn't, they'd be evicted; others needed money to eat or buy
medicine because a family member was ill, and so forth. During
the first strike my brothers weren't here in Tijuana yet, so I didn't
need much money to support myself.

The fact that many fellow strikers were married gave rise to a
lot of problems. Some husbands refused permission, and some
women had to go find work in another factory. But there were also
some who found work elsewhere in order to give their earnings to
those who needed it most. Many women had to work in stores, and
the majority of the guys worked as mechanics, so they alternated
between working and supporting the strike. There were people
who found good jobs, and they would donate part of their salary for
the rest of the strikers who had to support their families. That's
how we went about it, and we gained strength that way, even
though we were inexperienced.

With the first strike we won a number of concessions, above all,
the signing of a collective labor contract and the recovery of lost
wages, retroactive to the beginning of the strike. Another important fact is that the union was recognized.

The day we returned to work we were delighted. We realized
that we had won a lot, that we had gained something fair, and that
together we possessed a lot of strength. Before the strike we had
many problems with management, above all, with the supervisors.
Sometimes they suspended us. They dismissed us for arriving late,
for seeking personal concessions, or for errors affecting production,
but all that was unjust. Many times they had no reason to suspend
or lay us off. They treated us like dogs! Now that we had formed
the union and signed a collective bargaining agreement, everything
was different. After we formed the union, work was more to our
liking. It was easier to get personal time away from the job, and we
worked fewer hours.

With the union in place we had our first official meeting. Before
we formed the union we used to meet in the street because we had
no other place to go. After the union was recognized, the members
of CROC [Confederación Revolucionaria de Obreros y Campe-
sinos—Revolutionary Workers' and Peasants' Council] lent us their

meeting hall. We had union assemblies every two weeks, or more often if circumstances demanded. We held them one hour after the end of shift, to give the members time to eat and go pick up their children. Everyone had to sign the attendance book. As the meeting and discussions were beginning, we took advantage of the time to eat sandwiches or tacos to ease our hunger, because many of us didn't have time to eat. Some were exhausted from a hard day's work, and they slept sitting up during the meeting, with everything happening and the shouts of people involved in the discussion. There was also a lot of noise because mothers brought their children, and it's impossible to keep so many kids quiet. Other girls, instead of participating in the discussion, read magazines; some did nothing, but they didn't dare speak because they got embarrassed, they didn't like the feeling of being on the spot. By contrast, there were some who talked all the time and participated in everything, and others who expounded their opinions without reflection. The meetings lasted for two or three hours, and during that time they debated and discussed the situation of the labor union.

The Solidev Union is independent, and we are all very upstanding people, but still, we have to be careful, because wherever you are there are always slackers. Not everyone attended the first meetings. It was always the same people who went. We thought it was unfair, and we really got after people to participate and to assume the same rights and responsibilities. That was when we decided that everyone would sign in at every meeting, and that people would be fined for nonattendance.

Many argued that they couldn't attend because they had children to care for, because their spouses didn't allow it, or things of that nature. We didn't allow this to interfere, because we never would have done anything. People were allowed to miss only for exceptional reasons.

Fining people worked very well because it kept them from skipping meetings. I know it's disagreeable to have to be that way, but, unfortunately, many of us don't perform unless there's pressure. This is a rule, but in the union we are very flexible. We excused those who work somewhere else, and they always supported whatever we might have decided in the union. We also made allowances for those who arrived late because they had farther to go to pick up their children. Children were allowed, so no one had an excuse for missing meetings. We couldn't resolve the issue any other way.

A lot of women fail to see the advantages of belonging to a

union, but I worked in this factory when the union didn't exist, and I can assure you that we are much better off now. Before they didn't give us permission to leave work even to go to the doctor. They really got on us if we arrived late, and, if they felt like it, they would summarily suspend or fire us and never hear our reasons. We had to work overtime and the quotas were very demanding.

There are things that neither the union nor anyone else have been able to prevent. There are the famous blacklists that all the maquiladora managers have, where they record the names of dissident workers, all of us who created problems for the firms. If your name is on the list, they won't ever give you a job in the other maquiladoras. Those of us who work in Solidev will probably never be offered work elsewhere. Various fellow workers who were fired from Solidev sought work in other plants, and they were denied as soon as they gave their names. Obviously, they were on the blacklist. As someone said, they keep files on us.

They called us "rebellious" because we demanded our rights. A year after we formed the union, we called a strike to renew the collective bargaining agreement. Management was stupid to resist renewing the collective bargaining agreement, but we had organized well in advance against that contingency, and we held to our strike plan.

We began mobilizing a week before, collecting funds and handing out flyers. We prepared ourselves well so as to avoid the errors of our first experience, when we struck without being prepared. Fortunately, we didn't have to strike, because in the talks we resolved the problems and once again signed the contract, but this time for two years.

About three months before it was time to sign the collective bargaining agreement of 1982, the firm laid off some workers; about three days later they laid off forty-nine others and closed one department, saying there were no raw materials to work with. A new manager made this decision; he had worked with us for only a few months and, unlike the others, he was an ineffectual character. We couldn't allow them to run off those workers, because the move was intended to weaken the union, which had always served to protect job security. The union had guaranteed that the firm wouldn't lay us off out of the blue, as they do in other factories.

When we went to the final meeting before going out on the second strike, the assembly resolved that if we were agreed, we would strike in ten days. That left very little time to organize, but prior experience helped us a lot. We were all very fired up and nervous because we knew the burden that a strike created. Some of

During the strike the women still had to prepare meals for the other strikers, a job the men were never required to perform.

us were working on an outside project to create a child care center, because for those of us who are working mothers, it is a serious problem to have nowhere to leave your children while you're at work. We had to suspend the project for a while because we had to devote all our attention to the strike that awaited us.

The strike was called on April 13, 1982. We asked for reinstatement of the forty-nine laid-off workers, respect for the collective bargaining agreement, and a salary increase to offset the February 1982 currency devaluation.

We had reviewed the collective bargaining agreement the preceding August, at which time we negotiated a 20 percent salary increase, with an additional 5 percent beginning in February 1982. When the time came for the firm to begin paying the additional 5 percent, we initiated talks. In January 1982 the government had authorized a general raise of 33 percent in the minimum wage and professional salaries, and we pointed out to the firm that the 20 percent raise we had negotiated the previous August, plus the 5 percent they were to pay beginning in February, was less than the official government decree of January. So we proposed that the February increment should not be 5 percent, but more on the order of 15 to 20 percent.

We held talks with the company and they accepted our demands. The company decided to give us a raise in February: 20 percent for the workers with the lowest salaries, 15 percent for those with higher salaries. After we had arrived at that amount, there was another devaluation, so we demanded a further increase of 30 percent, the same amount agreed to by the federal authorities, but the company refused to concede that.

They told us that, because they had already agreed to certain terms, they could offer only a total increase of 30 percent. The union disagreed because that 30 percent merely reflected the devaluation's effective reduction of purchasing power. Because the company denied our demands, we were obliged to call a strike to defend our negotiated right to a raise in real terms and to protest the dismissal of our forty-nine fellow workers.

In our sealed demands we also used the occasion to demand fulfillment of various clauses in the collective bargaining agreement that were being violated. The company was saying that the forty-nine dismissals were not cause for a strike, because they had been let go before the strike began. What the company wanted was to finish off the union, and they devised every possible means to divide us and bring about our disintegration. Besides, how were we not going to demand the augmentation of salaries knowing that the products we make are sold for dollars, which for the firm has been a great arrangement, because they earn in dollars and pay us in pesos?

In fact, as Gabriela noted, the foreign firms benefited greatly from the currency devaluation. Prior to February 1982, Solidev Mexicana had a weekly payroll of about U.S.$22,000, but after the devaluation it paid out only U.S.$12,000. Hence, the devaluation constituted a weekly windfall of U.S.$10,000, apart from the savings on taxes, water, and electricity, all paid in Mexican currency:

We workers were affected by the devaluation, but for the owners it was a great deal. Here in Tijuana, and generally along the entire border, we have to buy a lot of American products—basic necessities—with prices marked in dollars. Every time there is a devaluation we buy fewer products; every time we poor people become poorer, and the rich become richer.

During the strike the manager tried to divide the union membership, offering money and better salaries on the condition that people leave the union. After ten days of striking, the Board of Conciliation and Arbitration [Junta de Conciliación y Arbitraje] declared the strike null and void.

We all had to present ourselves at work, and we were very demoralized. We considered going out on strike again, but we had to think it through carefully, because if the Board nullified it once again, that would be a severe blow to the union. The Board's decision left the manager feeling more powerful, and he treated us very badly, as badly as when we didn't have the union. He treated us increasingly harshly, and he refused to discuss or negotiate the violations of the collective bargaining agreement. Given his inflexibility, we decided that the best strategy would be to secure, at the very least, the compensation of our dismissed fellow workers.

The situation seemed to be good and the negotiations improved. Still, between September and October 1982, the owner began taking some of the machinery out of the factory. During that time, a fire broke out at the plant, but, curiously, only the administrative files were burned. During those months they really neglected the cleaning of the plant, and it began to look like an old warehouse. This seemed very fishy to all of us, because the manager was evidently not at all concerned about the plant. We began to suspect that they wanted to close it down, so we decided to post sentries

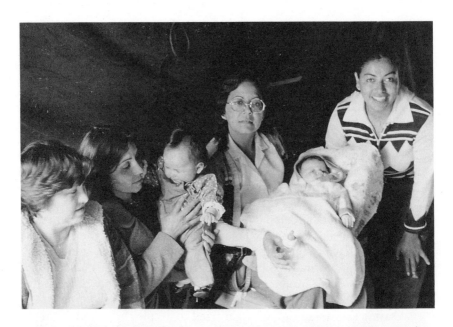

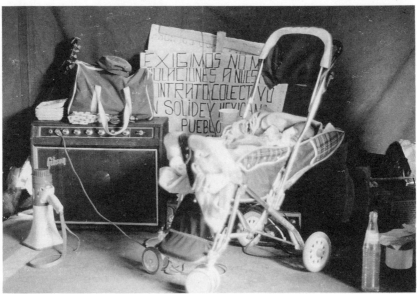

Children were never an impediment to participation in the strike.

The mutual support, including caring for each other's children, was ongoing during the strike and an unforgettable experience.

During the strike, there were moments of discouragement and fatigue.

Even when doing work that had no relation to their daily jobs, the women still participated with enthusiasm.

every afternoon, evening, and night to guard against their taking away any more machinery.

In November they took advantage of a moment when no sentries were there to remove the machinery in the department producing the Vinson product line, whose workers were the most combative. It's clear that they had been watching us for some time, because as soon as our fellow workers dropped their guard, the manager's men removed the machinery.

After that we all thought they weren't going to let us inside the plant, because we weren't going to have anything to work with. But they did allow us in without any problems, and we kept clocking in. We did almost no work, though, because we had nothing to work with. And in spite of everything, they kept paying us.

During that time, while we were hardly working, a reporter wrote an article saying that the Solidev workers were a bunch of slackers who weren't working. He took pictures of the people when they weren't doing anything. The reporter was almost certainly hired by the firm. All this was used against us, with the knowledge that we were not working precisely because the company didn't want us to, because we had nothing to work with.

They wanted people in Tijuana to think that we were lazy good-for-nothings and that we just wanted to stir up trouble because we were involved in leftist politics.

After a few days, just as we were to be paid for the week and collect the Christmas bonus, the owner's guards refused us entrance into the plant. The company said they would allow us to enter only if we repudiated our adviser,[3] the one who had supported us and struggled on our behalf since the formation of the union. He had always been honest and fair in his dealings. The managers said that the PSUM [Partido Socialista Unificado de México—Unified Socialist Party of Mexico] had infiltrated the union and that our adviser was a bad influence; we had to remove him if we wanted to keep our jobs.

We held a meeting, and the fear of losing our jobs obliged the majority of members to vote for our adviser's removal. It was thanks to him that we achieved so many things through the union. We all appreciated him and placed our confidence in him, but fear made many members believe that his leaving was best.

The owners told us that our adviser had to be a member of CROC, and that we had to register there. As we wanted to resolve the conflict, we did so. Then CROC recommended that we all affiliate with the PRI [Partido Revolucionario Institucional—Institutional Revolutionary Party],[4] telling us that by doing so we would convince U.S. investors to open the plant again.

How was it that they told us we should affiliate with the PRI, when the firm had told us that to counter political infiltration we should remove our adviser? With all that, the majority of us signed our PRI affiliation cards.

The first day of February 1983 they closed the plant permanently. They fooled us but good. We were all demoralized: the state government, the American owners, and the Mexican manager had united to do us in. They stopped at nothing to destroy the union. We pressured the Board of Conciliation and Arbitration to secure compensation, and after fighting around the clock, they gave us only 70 percent of what we were owed. This was an accomplishment in that the company had tried doggedly not to pay us anything.

We had a sort of fiesta to get together and discuss our experience and to send off those who were heading for the other side. We all felt very sad after so many years of working and struggling together. Spending all my life there for some good-for-nothing son of a bitch to come along and close the plant! We were all choked up,

which is what happens to you when you're angry and sad all at
once. Still, there is something that will always make us hold our
heads up high: we all learned, and we all made ourselves into po-
litically conscious people. None of us who were in the union are
the same as we were before. Now we know how to fight and demand our due. All that's left for us is to see where we're going to
work.

At present [1982], Gabriela is working in Los Angeles, California. Her
experience in the Solidev union invites us to reflect on the possibilities
and limitations of the independent labor union in Mexico. It is appropriate to note that, although this union was the only one of its type[5] in the
maquiladora industry in Tijuana, there are similar ones all over the
country.

In Tijuana unionization is rare: 5 percent in 1979. Labor is subordinated in the context of a declining demand for workers. There are
constant dismissals and threats (e.g., the blacklists), in conformity with
an organized structure linking the line boss, the supervisor, and the
manager, exercised via opportunistic hiring policies and control of the
mass media. This situation has fueled growing discontent among unionized workers, whether members of official or independent unions.

Still, the spirit of independent unionism persists in the maquiladoras,
although most such efforts have not had positive outcomes. The only
movements to end in formation of a union were those at Crescent in
Zacatecas and Solidev Mexicana in Tijuana (Carrillo 1982). These two
exceptional experiences have had similar outcomes. With respect to the
Solidev union, it is important to note that, even though the majority of
workers were women, only a small number of them served on the
union's executive committee or participated in general union decision
making.

The claims and demands specific to women were few. It was often
forgotten that women, in the context of their specific problematic, have
their own set of needs, which do not always coincide with the traditional
demands of labor. Any policy or approach to organizing that excludes or
fails to take into account the interests and needs of the largest part of the
membership will be futile. Thus, if the problematic of women is not
taken into consideration, no effort to organize the maquiladoras will
achieve wide-ranging gains. It is necessary to frame specific demands,
because society is divided along both class and gender lines.

In general terms, the experience gained by the workers at Solidev is of
considerable importance. Despite being left without work—after a
debilitating struggle—they have learned about organizing and how to

confront the owners. Now these workers can communicate their experience to their fellows and awaken an interest in and eagerness for organizing as the only means to confront capital.

Notes

1. The firm began operations with approximately three hundred workers, but its workforce continued growing until it reached fifteen hundred in 1974.

2. The official government entity for arbitrating and resolving all labor disputes—individual and collective. Labor unions are also registered with this board.

3. The adviser was a labor lawyer who did not work for the company.

4. The Partido Revolucionario Institucional (Institutional Revolutionary Party), since its emergence during the Mexican Revolution, has ruled the nation's political process.

5. This union, in spite of being affiliated with the official labor unions, was very active in its demands. It worked with local, national, and U.S. labor groups and was democratic, a rarity in the maquiladora unions.

8.

By Way of Conclusion

Without a doubt, the life stories presented here pose many questions that deserve careful analysis for their relevance to a study of the working class. The narratives illustrate what women confront, day in and day out, after being incorporated into the production process.

The first point deserving special attention is that the fragmentation of the production process prevents female workers from developing an understanding of the total process. In other words, regardless of how long a woman is employed in a maquiladora, she will never have the opportunity to become a skilled worker. Thus, she will always be a cheap source of labor. Her chances of advancement on the salary and position scales are practically nil. Her experience as a worker, should she leave the firm or be dismissed and seek other employment, hardly constitutes a recommendation, because her work was so specialized that, despite the skills she acquired, she would find another position like it only with difficulty.

The same specialization of tasks to which she is conditioned squelches her creativity and dehumanizes her to a great degree as it subordinates, oppresses, and envelops her in a whirlwind of endless work. Added to this, on a daily basis she confronts the instability and insecurity of her employment status and the relative and absolute reduction of her salary. Obliged to meet a specified production quota, she is subject to demanding and routine manual tasks and work rhythms whose monotony produces alienation. She endures inadequate workplace safety, the hazards of occupational illness, and absurd regulations that limit even her trips to the bathroom.

The abundant labor supply on the Tijuana frontier has been a decisive factor in enabling maquiladoras to continually refine their employment policies. In this way the women must meet more requirements: they must be young and pretty, have a primary school certificate, and prove permanent residence in Tijuana, among other things. Yet, depending on what the maquiladora produces, variations on the classic occupational structure can be found. Hence, there are maquiladoras that hire women over thirty years of age, heads of family, and single or married mothers who have not finished primary school. These women bear a greater economic responsibility and, because of their social situation, are more dependent on their salaries. These determinants pressure female laborers to endure all manner of working conditions and make it difficult for them to participate in any prospective movement to assert worker rights.

Variations in the occupational structure aside, the problem of employment instability persists precisely because of the tendency of the maquiladoras to continually replace personnel. This policy is so firmly entrenched that the average length of female employment in the maquiladora does not exceed five years. There is considerable elasticity in the labor market due to the regular incorporation of new elements and the elimination of others, all of which contributes to steady growth in the unemployment rate. Maquiladoras generally dismiss women older than twenty-five or thirty years of age and replace them with younger women, from whom greater productivity is anticipated. This rotation of female workers is made possible by the vast reserve workforce and the role of maquiladoras in creating a reserve army of labor that can be used or discarded in accord with the industry's interests and needs.

As the life histories show, the maquiladoras design and implement a range of political-ideological mechanisms and controls that reinforce the companies' employment policies with the aim of maintaining a reserve army of labor. The working woman in the maquiladora is convinced that she has been hired for her abilities, yet she knows perfectly well that she will be replaced in short order. Owner-worker relations, on the other hand, are veiled in mystery, where the owner is a benevolent dictator whose privileges include even the sexual exploitation of female workers. The owner thus perceives the working woman not only as docile, able, attentive, and patient, but also as a sexual object.

Finally, it is necessary to emphasize the global character that productive processes assume in the maquiladoras, and the advantages and difficulties this poses for workers' struggles. On one side, the presence of female workers at the negotiation tables—when this occurs—is diluted because decision-making processes are centralized in the firms' headquarters and because management's representatives have relatively little power and authority to alter maquiladora production policy locally. Under these conditions, the workers' struggle is hindered, and in the short term their influence appears to be reduced by not having a hand in every stage of production. This undercuts the movement's power, for the ability to halt production at any stage would control the industry. Notwithstanding, the internationalization of productive processes, of capital, and of the division of labor favors a greater degree of working-class political consciousness-raising, encourages an appeal to other workers beyond the border region, and demands a structural transformation of the entire economic and productive system.

It is also evident that the women of the maquiladoras, as members of a subordinated class, still have only limited autonomy in the triple standard of consciousness, organization, and mobilization. Still, they begin to share their specific problems as members of a socioeconomic class and as women, and they discover that they are not alone. Both formally and informally they begin meeting to discuss the exploitation to which they are subject in the factories, the common hazards to their health, and working conditions, including the domination they suffer at the hands of supervisors, managers, husbands, and children. In their mutual encounter women have forged support structures and networks to sustain themselves in the workplace and have demonstrated a degree of organization. There are instances of women who join to pay one of their fellow workers the same salary she would make in the factory, but to take care of the children of those who contribute money. This form of organization results from and illustrates the fact that the problematic of working women is specific.

A good many of women's limitations in terms of achieving a broader degree of organization and mobilization are closely linked to that convergence of contradictions that resides and unfolds in the lives of each and every female maquiladora worker. On the one hand, they are grateful and feel indebted to the firm for having given them a job:

> Perhaps it seems that I exaggerate, but when I began working in the maquiladora it gave me a feeling of great happiness, as though I had overcome my past. It was the moment in which God heard me and changed my life. I could forget about what was behind me . . .

On the other hand, as this working woman tells us,

> in the maquiladoras they exploit us a lot; all the livelong day they keep us working as rapidly as a machine, and without any protection. The conditions are so bad that we soon become ill, and then because we are no longer of service to them, they run us off with impunity. We don't have any guarantees.

This is the great contradiction that pervades all the cases examined here, cases that represent a broad sector of the working population in the maquiladora industries. It is in precisely this contradiction that the foundations of labor organization must be sought.

Appendices

Work History

1. Name of the company where employed.
2. Address of the company.
3. Company's type of business.
4. Age of the company.
5. Name and location of company's headquarters or main office.
6. Interviewee's age.
7. Interviewee's sex.
8. Interviewee's marital status.
9. Number of children.
10. Where do you leave your children while you are working?
11. If your children do not live with you, with whom do they live?
12. How old were you when you had your first child?
13. What is the highest grade of school you have completed?
14. Have you taken other classes or courses?
15. If so, for how long?
16. Why did you stop studying?
17. Where were you born? (state, city, village, hamlet)
18. How long have you lived in Tijuana?
19. Where did you grow up? (state, city, village, hamlet)
20. Why did you migrate to Tijuana?
21. With whom did you migrate to Tijuana? (relationship, age, sex, occupation, level of education, place of employment)
22. At what age did you begin working (occupational history of migrants)? Where? Until what age? Salary? Why did you stop working?
23. Other places you have resided for over six months.
24. Once in Tijuana, where and when did you begin to work? Occupation? Place of employment? Salary? Length of employment? Principal job activity? Why did you change your place of work?
25. How long do you anticipate continuing to work?

26. How did you learn about the availability of work in the maquiladoras?

27. What does your father do for a living? Occupation? Place of employment?

28. What does your mother do for a living? Occupation? Place of employment?

29. What does your husband or partner do for a living? Occupation? Place of employment?

30. What does/do your child(ren) do for a living? Occupation(s)? Place(s) of employment?

31. How long have you been working for your current employer?

32. Number of workers employed there.

33. How many male employees?

34. How many female employees?

35. Interviewee's job description at the maquiladora.

36. Daily production standard or quota.

37. How much do you earn per week?

38. Do you have a permanent job?

39. Is the plant where you work unionized?

40. What qualifications did the company specify for employment?

41. Have you had a work-related illness or been injured in a work-related accident?

42. Specification of the preceding.

43. Duration of disability.

44. What kind of benefits do you have at the company where you are employed?

45. How many people ordinarily live in your home?

46. Who are they? Relationship? Age? Sex? Marital status? Year in school? Occupation? Place of employment?

47. Among those who live with you, who contributes to household expenses? Person(s) and amounts(s).

48. How do you budget your salary? Transportation? Meals at work? Savings? Loan payments? How much do you send to your family (if a migrant)? How much do you give to your mother? Sent in care of?

49. How much do you spend on the following: Lights? Gas? Electricity? Water? Food? Clothing? Furniture? Medical care? Children's education? Transportation or gasoline? Entertainment?

50. What do you ordinarily do after work?

51. Who is responsible for housecleaning?

52. Who cooks? Washes the dishes? Sweeps and dusts? Washes the clothes? Runs household errands?

53. Which of the following do you have at home? Bathroom? Sewage system? Hot water? Radio? Record player? Television? Telephone?

54. Do you own a car?
55. Do you belong to any groups or organizations?
56. What does the group/organization do?
57. What do you think of the maquiladoras?
58. Why do you think that they prefer women as maquiladora workers?
59. Do you get together with workers from the maquiladora outside of work? What do you do together?
60. Has your life changed since you began working in the maquiladora?
61. What are the advantages and disadvantages of working in the maquiladora?
62. What kind of work would you like to be doing in five years?
63. Do you think you can achieve that objective?
64. What kind of work or career would you like your children to have?
65. How do you spend your weekends?
66. How did you spend your free time before you started working at the maquiladora?
67. If you had money right now, what would you like to do?
68. What neighborhood do you live in?

Interviewer's observations.

Name and address of the interviewee.

Thematic Guide for Eliciting Interviewee's Life History

Place of origin.
Birth date.
Parents' occupations at time of interviewee's birth.
Family economic status.
Social, economic, and cultural characteristics of place of origin.
Family circumstances.
Number of family members.
Relationship of family members.
Family traditions.
Family anecdotes and deaths.
The role of women in the home.
Life perspective of interviewee and family members.
Type of work and activities of interviewee in the home and community.
Knowledge of life on the Mexico-U.S. border.
Knowledge of the maquiladoras.
First work experience (if first job was not in the place of origin, begin with migration).
Migration.

Reasons for migration.

Reasons for deciding to migrate to Tijuana.

Difficulties in the migration experience.

Interviewee's images of the destination.

Perspectives and feelings about migration.

Work history in the maquiladoras.

Description of work inside the maquiladoras.

Description of the different posts held in the maquiladoras.

How interviewee became aware of maquiladora work and basis of decision to work there.

Opinion of the maquiladoras before starting to work there.

Where interviewee learned the tasks performed in the maquiladora.

Type of contractual arrangements (did the worker sign a contract upon being hired, and, if so, what type?).

Qualifications required to secure work in the maquiladoras.

Adaptation to work.

Adaptation to and problems with other workers.

Problems encountered on first starting to work (feelings; overcoming problems).

Did you think you would work only temporarily?

Did you think your life was going to change when you started working in the maquiladora?

What advantages and disadvantages did working in the maquiladora offer?

Information about the source of work.

Knowledge about the work process.

Knowledge about what the company produces.

Knowledge of the company's organizational structure.

Knowledge of the market.

Raw materials and inputs (source, volume, etc.).

Importance of the establishment in relation to other companies (competition).

Company ownership.

Managerial levels.

Participation and promotion of nonproductive activities (sports, recreational, social).

Work process.

Work day, work week, and work month. Calculate the work regime in terms of hours per week.

Work schedule, lunch hour. Worker sanctions.

Shifts (night shift, extra-long days, overtime). Reasons for working, production, pay, problems, and schedule variations by:

department
variations in the pace of work
new administrative and organizational forms of work
daily work routine
transportation to and from work
means utilized
duration
cost
sanctions for arriving late.
Work preliminaries (clock-in, clothing change, machinery preparation, inventory of tools or work accumulated the previous day).
Description of work.
Aspects of production and tasks performed. Stability and variation of the same.
Responsibilities and obligations.
Interviewee's role in the production process:
from whom material is received
in what state
what is done to it
with whose assistance or using what tools or machinery
where the material goes next
what is done to it then.
Difficulties and problems in the work regime (solutions).
Workplace risks, tiredness, fatigue, monotony, tedium, etc.
Thoughts during the work day. Attitudes.
Presence of other workers who perform the same tasks.
Work competency.
Standards of production (quotas), increases and decreases. Conveyor belt, assembly line, and individual work. Determination of the number of units made in a day.
Machinery and technology.
Tools and machines used in the production unit.
Tools and machines used in the department.
Tools and machines used by the worker.
Use of conveyor belts, rails, or other means to accelerate the work pace.
Obsolete machinery. Causes of technological evolution.
Who, when, and where: maintenance, cleaning, repair of machinery. How this knowledge is conveyed. Who does the work. Gender, qualifications.
Ownership of tools used in production.
Perceptions of technical evolution and its repercussions for work.
Innovations of the workers.

Worker relations in the maquiladora.
Nature of relations between female workers.
Nature of relations between female and male workers.
Nature of relations between female workers and male superiors.
Life outside the maquiladora.
Activities engaged in before or after work in the maquiladora.
Description of the "double work day" of women. Schedule of work in the
    home.
Recreational activities. Types of diversion, expenditures for the same.
Budgeting of salary.
Worker organization.

Bibliography

Amin, Samir
1977   *¿Cómo funciona el capitalismo? El intercambio desigual y la ley del valor.* Mexico City: Siglo XXI.
Aranda, Clara Eugenia, et al., eds.
1976   *La mujer: explotación, lucha, liberación.* Mexico City: Editorial Nuestro Tiempo.
Aranquren, José Luis
1977   *Erotismo y liberación.* Barcelona: Editorial Ariel.
Artous, Antoine
1978   *Los orígenes de la opresión de la mujer (sistema capitalista y opresión de la mujer).* Barcelona: Fontamara.
Bagu, Sergio, et al.
1983   *Teoría marxista de las clases sociales.* Mexico City: Universidad Autónoma Metropolitana.
Beauvoir, Simone de
1975   *El segundo sexo.* Buenos Aires: Siglo XXI.
Bebel, August
1980   *La mujer; en el pasado, en el presente, en el porvenir.* 3d ed. Barcelona: Editorial Fontamara.
Bernstein, Alan, et al.
1977   *Silicon Valley: Paradise or Paradox? The Impact of the High Technology Industry on Santa Clara County.* Mountain View, Calif.: Pacific Studies Center.
Braverman, Harry
1975   *Trabajo y capital monopolista.* Mexico City: Ed. Nuestro Tiempo.
Broyelle, Claudie
1975   *La mitad del cielo. El movimiento de la liberación de la mujer china.* 2d ed. Madrid: Siglo XXI.
Bustamante, Jorge A.
1980   La conceptualización y programación del desarrollo de la zona frontera norte. Paper presented at the Reunión de Universidades de México–Estados Unidos sobre Estudios Fronterizos, La Paz, Baja California Sur (February 27–29).

Bustamante, Jorge A., et al.
1975   El programa fronterizo de maquiladoras: observaciones para una evaluación. *Foro Internacional* 16(2): 183–204.
Bustamante, Jorge A., and Francisco Malagamba
1980   *México–Estados Unidos: bibliografía general sobre estudios fronterizos.* Mexico City: El Colegio de México.
Calderón, Ernesto C.
1981   Las maquiladoras de los países centrales que operan en el tercer mundo. In *Lecturas del CEESTEM*, pp. 72–100. Mexico City: Centro de Estudios Económicos y Sociales del Tercer Mundo.
Carrillo, Jorge
1982   Cierre de fábricas: La conservación del empleo prioritario. In *Crítica Política* (October): 55–56.
Carrillo, Jorge, and Alberto Hernández
1981   Las maquiladoras en la frontera: algunas consideraciones para su evaluacón. Paper presented at the Research Seminar on U.S. Relations. Center for United States–Mexican Studies. San Diego: University of California, San Diego.
1982a   *La mujer obrera en la industria maquiladora: el caso de Ciudad Juárez.* Mexico City: Universidad Nacional Autónoma de México.
1982b   Sindicatos y control en las plantas maquiladoras fronterizas. *Investigación Económica* 161: 105–155.
1985   *Mujeres fronterizas en la industria maquiladora.* Mexico City: Secretaría de Educación Pública, Centro de Estudios Fronterizos del Norte de México.
Carrillo, Jorge, and Mónica Jasís
1982   La salud y la mujer obrera en las plantas maquiladoras: el caso de Tijuana. Paper presented at the annual meeting of the Society for Applied Anthropology (March), San Diego, Calif.
Chávez, Elisa
1981   Las empresas matrices de las maquiladoras mexicanas: dos estudios de caso de la industria del vestido. In *Lecturas del CEESTEM*, pp. 61–71. Mexico City: Centro de Estudios Económicos y Sociales del Tercer Mundo.
Coriat, Benjamín
1979   *L'Atelier et le chronométre.* Paris: Ed. Christian Bourgeois.
Costa, Dalla M., and Selma James
1979   *El poder de la mujer y la subversión de la comunidad.* 3d ed. Mexico City: Siglo XXI.
de Leonardo, Margarita
1976   La mujer y las clases sociales en México. In *La mujer: explotación, lucha y liberación*, Clara Eugenia Aranda et al., eds., pp. 1–58. Mexico City: Editorial Nuestro Tiempo.
Dos Santos, T.
1979   La corporación multinacional. In *Problemas del subdesarrollo latinoamericano*, pp. 126–168. 5th ed. Mexico City: Editorial Nuestro Tiempo.

Driscoll, Barbara
1996   *Me voy pa' Pensilvania por no andar en la vagancia.* Mexico City: Consejo Nacional para la Cultura y las Artes, Universidad Nacional Autónoma de México.
Eisenstein, Zillah R.
1980   *Patriarcado, capitalismo y feminismo socialista.* Mexico City: Siglo XXI.
El-Sanabary, Nagat M., ed.
1983   *Women and Work in the Third World: The Impact of Industrialization and Global Economic Interdependence.* Proceedings of the Center for the Study of Education and Advancement of Women (June). Berkeley: University of California.
Frobel, Folker, Jurgen Heinrichs, and Otto Kreye
1981   *La nueva división internacional del trabajo: para estructurar en los países industrializados e industrialización de los países en desarrollo.* 2d ed. Mexico City: Siglo XXI.
Galarza, Ernesto
1964   *Merchants of Labor: The Mexican Bracero Story.* Charlotte & Santa Barbara: McNally & Loftin.
Gambrill, Mónica Claire
1981   La fuerza del trabajo en las maquiladoras; resultados de una encuesta y algunas hipótesis interpretativas. In *Lecturas del CEESTEM,* pp. 7–60. Mexico City: Centro de Estudios Económicos y Sociales del Tercer Mundo.
Green, Susan S.
1980   Silicon Valley's Women Workers: A Theoretical Analysis of Sex-regration in the Electronic Industry Labor Market. Paper presented at Impact of Transnational Interactions Project Culture Learning Institute (July), Honolulu.
Iglesias Prieto, Norma
1982   *Marco conceptual de la comprensión de la utilización de mujeres en la industria maquiladora.* Tijuana, Baja California: Centro de Estudios Fronterizos del Norte de México.
Instituto Nacional de Estadística, Geografía e Informática (INEGI)
1996   *Banco de datos sobre la industria maquiladora.* Mexico City.
Kollontay, Alejandra
1977   *El marxismo y la nueva moral sexual (teoría y praxis).* Mexico City: Grijalbo.
Lenin, V.
1975   *Acerca de los sindicatos.* Mexico City: Editorial Progreso.
Linhart, Robert
1979   *De cadenas y de hombres.* Mexico City: Siglo XXI.
Lugo, Carmen
1977   La mujer y el trabajo: bibliografía selecta. *FEM* 1 (3) (April–June): 64–66.
Mandel, Ernest
1978   *Alienación y emancipación del proletariado.* Barcelona: Fontamara.

Marini, Mario Mauro
1978   *Dialéctica de la dependencia.* 9th ed. Mexico City: Siglo XXI.
1983   *Subdesarrollo y revolución.* Mexico City: Siglo XXI.
Mattelart, Armand
1978   *La comunicación masiva en el proceso de la liberación.* 6th ed. Mexico
        City: Siglo XXI.
Mattelart, Michele
1978   Las mujeres y el orden de la crisis. In *Comunicación e ideologías de la
        seguridad,* pp. 9–39. Barcelona: Editorial Anagrama.
Moro, Martín, et al.
1978   *Control y lucha del movimiento obrero.* Mexico City: Editorial Nuestro
        Tiempo.
Muñoz, María Elena, and Guadalupe Murayama M.
1979   Las obreras de la industria maquiladora. *FEM* 1 (3) (April–June): 40–46.
Murayama M., Guadalupe, and María Elena Muñoz
1979   Empleo de la mano de obra feminina en la industria de la exportación.
        Cuadernos Agrarios 4(9).
Neffa, Julio César
1990   *El proceso de trabajo y la economía de tiempo: contribución al análisis
        crítico de K. Marx, F. W. Taylor y H. Ford.* Buenos Aires: Ed. Humanitas-
        CREDAL.
Paz, Octavio
1982   *El laberinto de la soledad.* Mexico City: Fondo de Cultura Económica.
Poulantzas, Nicos
1976   *Poder político y clases sociales en el estado capitalista.* Mexico City:
        Siglo XXI.
Randall, Margaret
1982   La mujer: especificidad de su problemática. *El Día* (October 25): 4.
Redd, Evelyn
1980   *Sexo contra sexo o clase contra clase.* Barcelona: Editorial Fontamara.
Sau, Victoria
1981   *Un diccionario feminista.* Barcelona: Editorial Icaria.
Secretaría de Programación y Presupuesto (SPP)
1980   *Estadisticas sobre la industria maquiladora.* Mexico City.
Tse, Christina
1980   The Invisible Control: Management Control of Workers in a U.S.
        Electronics Company (mimeo). N.p.: Center for the Progress of People.

Index